Dynamic Discernment

Dynamic Discernment

Reason, Emotion, and Power
in Change Leadership

Sarah B. Drummond

the pilgrim press

since 1640

The Pilgrim Press, 700 Prospect Avenue, Cleveland, Ohio 44115

thepilgrimpress.com

© 2019 by Sarah B. Drummond

Printed in the United States of America on acid-free paper.

23 22 21 20 19   5 4 3 2 1

Cataloging-in-Publication Data can be found online at the Library of Congress.

ISBN 978-0-8298-2045-4

Contents

Introduction   1

1: How We Think about Change   15

2: Reason   41

3: Emotion   83

4: Power   117

5: Discernment on the Leadership Terrain   151

Acknowledgments   173

Bibliography   174

Dedication

To my mother, Jacqueline J. Birmingham,
whose ticking typewriter
—to which I woke up every morning—
taught me:
do what you love, and write about it.

Introduction

A young, gifted staff member from a distinguished congregation came to see me at the advice of his supervisor for some vocational discernment. Kyle[1] had come to the church straight out of business school and wanted to make a difference in people's lives. He had started to think that ordained ministry or higher education administration might be a good next direction. I thought we would talk about matters of call and clergy and career, but it became apparent quickly that Kyle had something else on his mind: he felt that a member of the ministry team at his congregation needed to go, and he needed to be the one to show her the door. Knowing I had a good relationship with his supervisor, he wanted my advice about how to make his case.

Kyle went on to regale me with stories of the gross incompetence of the member of the ministry team whose job he felt he—or anyone, really—could do better. She never showed up for anything where she would not be the star. She buttered up influential people in the congregation and sucked up to her superiors but treated staff members who were lower than her on the food chain with disinterest and disdain. After what seemed like an unending list of complaints, Kyle shared with me his plan for how he would engineer the minister's demise and departure. I stopped him right there.

Not because I was bored with the story or because I did not believe him. Not because I did not care about him or felt the topic

---

[1] Not his real name. Except where first and last names are used to identify a person, first names only are used to identify someone who remains anonymous.

to be inappropriate for a mentoring conversation. Not because he is a man and his nemesis a woman. I held up my red, octagonal sign because Kyle clearly did not get it: his agenda was doomed to fail. Whether or not his colleague was competent made no difference, and nobody would care whether he was right. What mattered was that she was the one in the position of power and was evidently good at managing up. She was beloved by those whose love she needed. My advice to Kyle was that he needed to forget about her and focus on his own call, goals, values, and work ethic. Evidently, my advice came too late. His coup attempt was already in the offing. He was gone by month's end.

I am familiar with a church with a long history of sexual misconduct on the part of clergy—at least two ministers, spanning more than sixty years of the church's history. After the departure of the most recent abusive pastor, the church's treasurer was found to have stolen some money from the coffers. She had been a lifelong member of the church, found herself in dire financial straits, and did a bad thing. She was removed from her role, of course, and never returned to the church. She had taken some money, abused her position and the church's trust in her, and since trust was such a messy matter in the church already, she was cast out for life.

The clergy abuser's misdeeds were never taken seriously by the congregation, although the denomination held him accountable after he left his post and was seeking other ministry opportunities. The treasurer who stole was treated as a pariah in her own community, reputation destroyed. Does this dynamic make sense, where the vulnerable doer of wrong is vilified, and the powerful doer of wrong whose misconduct poisoned the well is not held accountable for decades? Of course it does not make sense, but I am betting it does not surprise us either.

What do these two anecdotes have in common? They demonstrate how many different forces are at work in a crisis, controversy, or change in a faith community. They highlight the dynamics of change that every leader must navigate with discerning wisdom: dynamic discernment. If we understand "dynamic" to be a noun, then we imagine this book will be about the discernment of dynamics in communities, and we would be correct. If we understand "dynamic" to be an adjective, the meaning likewise holds true, while turning on a different edge: discerning dynamically. This book considers how leaders can nimbly draw from a repertoire of practices depending on their read of a given moment's needs. I invite you to reflect on what is at stake for you as a reader as you consider your community's dynamics as they relate to change, and how you as a leader must adapt, moment by moment, to those dynamics. Adapting does not make a leader weak, peripatetic, or even inconsistent. The leader who cannot adapt cannot lead without burning out or losing their mind.

I am blessed to have been exposed to change as a dynamic, rather than a "problem," early in my ministry. I had been an ordained minister and educational administrator for a handful of years when I began a doctoral program in Urban Education at the University of Wisconsin–Milwaukee. As a member of and minister in the United Church of Christ, I knew something about how a community had to be brought along, gradually and carefully, when attempting something new. I understood that change imposed from on high was unlikely to succeed, and I had abundant examples from my own church and ministry to back that up.

Until I took a course on program planning and evaluation with Professor William Kritek, however, where change theory was central to the curriculum, I did not have words for what I had experienced and observed. An interdisciplinary field connected to business, psychology, and sociology, change theory gave me a language that has led to some of the most fascinating conversations of my ministry. Those conversations have evolved as I have gathered new experiences, and as the field has become more nuanced and sophisticated. Those new experiences included serving a campus ministry that was at death's door but that possessed the resources needed for a turnaround: a facility, a budget, a devoted board. That experience propelled me into theological education, as I discovered a passion for not just working with students but helping them learn to be ministerial leaders.

The seminary I was called to serve was already thinking about major change—merger? closure? relocation?—years before I arrived, so I entered a conversation about the need for change while it was already unfolding. That said, my changing roles at Andover Newton Theological School, moving from faculty and field education to academic affairs, gave me numerous perspectives on how constituents react to change depending on what is at stake for them. I represented the school's academic interests in seven different partnership negotiations before one came about that has worked: to move the seminary onto dry ground as an embedded seminary in a university. With all the benefits that come with a strong and secure base, the costs have been high as well, including the toll taken on the human spirit by chronic confusion giving way to a sense of loss of place. I have taken to introducing myself in professional gatherings this way: "Hi, I'm Sarah. I'm from Andover Newton, which we've recently renamed 'It's Complicated.'"

In my first foray into the study of program planning and evaluation, I was taught change leadership as a step-by-step method for bringing a community along, explaining a vision and what needed to happen to get there. I was taught to assume that those I would lead are reasonable people. I had to look to other fields altogether, such as emotional systems and liberation theology, to understand the other—and often more powerful—dynamics at work in faith communities. Is this because change theory is inherently incomplete? That the interdisciplinary social science approach to institutional change was lacking? Perhaps, at the time, yes.

As I have continued to study change during these twenty-plus years, remarkably I have found that even change is changing. I have seen dramatic shifts in the language we use for the role of the leader in bringing about change. I have witnessed trust eroding in institutions, which means that the leaders in them experience intense scrutiny at every turn. I have seen resistance movements fail to bring about lasting cultural change because they lacked clear goals and focused energies; absent clarity or focus, such movements have failed to penetrate the corridors of power. As I have taught courses on change theory, I have yet to come across a survey of the varied lenses—rational, emotional, and liberationist—that can be used to describe a situation with more than "It's complicated." I wrote this book because I have come to believe that a shared vocabulary for describing change dynamics helps leaders to work together rather than at odds with one another.

How much conflict, stagnation, and decline in our churches has resulted not from different ideas of *what* changes needed to take place, but rather conflicting assumptions about *how* change happens? Imagine if leaders could look at a new idea from numerous perspectives and understand both the issues and each other. Those who take pleasure in analyzing what is going wrong in their churches could have more interesting conversations over their Sunday brunches. Those who take on the mantle of leadership could have more satisfying experiences, recognizing where they can have a real impact while sparing themselves disappointment where such impact is unlikely.

Throughout the history of God's interaction with creation, we see God providing the resources needed to face that which is uncertain and new. When God places us in situations we cannot face on our own, God gives us the tools we need. I felt called by God to write this book in order to put something—or some things—new in each reader's leadership toolbox. When we face that which might overwhelm us, we can use these tools to examine its component parts with the hope that, by not ignoring varied dynamics and not taking them on all at once, we can lead rather than find ourselves in despair.

In the pages that follow, expect abundant examples, exercises, and case studies. These tools honor the ways in which people learn, and because they are designed for groups as well as individuals, the tools acknowledge that the quest for a just and loving world is inherently communal. "Dynamic" signals movement among forces that interact with each other in the context of an evolving community. "Discernment" reminds us that, as we seek to change communities and institutions, our ultimate goal is to make them more like what God—rather than what we—imagines them to be.

At the time of my writing this book, the president of the United States is Donald Trump. He introduced the United States to "fake news," a term he uses to describe the words of his critics, when fact-checkers generally find that only about 25 percent of the so-called facts President Trump cited during his campaign were accurate. President Trump built a base of support through his capacity to conduct an orchestra of emotion in a symphony of discontent. His power, derived from wealth rather than wisdom, placed a higher premium on his financial successes than his clearly flawed capacity to reason. Ten years ago, a book on the ways in which reason and emotion and power all play into organizational dynamics amidst change would have had to persuade the reader why reason alone is not enough. During a Trump presidency, making the argument that reason still matters at all is the new challenge. Emotion and power, in this political moment, are everything.

I first studied change theory in a time when reason, making sense, and getting a community to see the light were primary. Now, reason is only part—and an ever-shrinking one—of the leader's challenge. Here is the good news: this book recognizes that multiple forces are at work when change happens in communities, but even though more than one dynamic is at work, chaos does not reign. Change dynamics can be analyzed and largely understood when we employ a variety of tools. As the saying goes, "When all you have is a hammer, everything looks like a nail." We need more than hammers in our leadership toolboxes.

When human beings face that which seems overwhelmingly complex, a series of possible reactions can ensue. We become discouraged and overwhelmed, and thus we opt out. Opting out can take the form of a leader withdrawing, even at times presenting their withdrawal as something that is good for the community. "It's really their decision," says the leader whose community is discerning a future during difficult times. "*They* have to do what *they* want." Or we decide that things must be simpler than they appear. Getting a headache from the complex array of people and their dynamics in community, we choose to paint over situations in black and white. If one interpretation of a leadership challenge is right, we conclude that all others must be wrong. We make *ad hominem* generalizations, saying that complaints coming from a particular person cannot be worthy of attention because of who that person is. "There goes Nelly again," we say, "Always trying to stir up trouble." We dismiss that which does not conform to our oversimplified analysis as sentiments that come from a lack of knowledge, or even a lack of faithfulness.

Opting out or painting a complex community simplistically are not useful practices for leaders or their communities. Three alternative dispositions for leaders amidst change—"sense-making," "separate-yet-togetherness," and "liberationist"—are ways in which leaders can bring together reason, emotion, and power without allowing any one of those dynamics to stealthily scuttle a change initiative. Pulling back or oversimplifying are both tempting stances, truly. They seem like good options when a person does not know what to do; they are natural when no alternative stances are available. This book not only promotes these more adequate stances but recommends practices for cultivating them, readying them for service when times demand them.

The physics of institutional change are worthy of their own glossary of terms as this book begins. First, "dynamic" is used to suggest movement rather than stagnation. It also suggests more than one party is involved in a change. Even in a conversation between two people, a dynamic is at work where the two bring more than the sum of their parts to a conversation. If one is having a bad day, if the other is harboring old resentments, the dynamic between them will reflect these negativities. A group's dynamic is only partly related to the topic on which they are focused; the unspoken vibe that shapes the dynamic can turn the most straightforward problem-solving conversation into a hotly contested debate.

The words "iterative" and "dialectic" describe the ways in which we play off one another in communities. Iterative interactions are ones where our engagements are habitual and toward a mutual goal, but not necessarily transformative. The manager works with an employee to set goals. The employee seeks to meet those goals. At certain intervals, the employee and manager revisit those goals. Where the employee has fallen short, the question under discussion is, "Did the employee miss the mark, or was this the wrong goal?" An iterative process is healthy and important in leadership.

Dialectics refer to iterative engagements that lead to transformation. Consider a meaningful interaction between two people who know each other only casually. They find themselves in a conversation about something personal, say, their fathers. One shares his story with the other. The listener then shares hers. But her story is different from having heard her conversation partner's story; if she had spoken first rather than second, her story might have been different. She has been changed by what she has heard. Perhaps she is bolder because of her conversation partner's modeling or has thought to name details she might not otherwise have considered important. Then her story changes her listener as he replies with further information or reflection. Dialectical change suggests not just patterned repetition, but transformation and growth.

Why are these terms—dynamics, iterative processes, dialectics—important at the start of a book like this? Because people can and do change, just not in ways that are easy to see, understand, label, or describe in generalizations. Our very theology of resurrection in the Christian tradition is enough to tell us that transformation happens not just at the threshold between life and death but many, many times over the course of a lifetime. Even if people do not fundamentally change, which some believe and others disbelieve, a dynamic can almost always change, and, thus, so can a community.

A final note about vocabulary: I come from a tradition that defines leadership with a flat hierarchy in mind. In the United Church of Christ, lay leaders hold power in ways that might surprise those from faith traditions where clergy and bishops hold more sway. For that reason, my model of leadership is multidimensional. In some settings, I am a leader; in other settings, I am led. In my church, I am part leader and part member, but never quite a follower. Therefore, this book is written with an idea that everyone is a leader somewhere, and thus the concepts of reason, emotion, and power in leading change will make sense to all in some part of their lives. As my first book *Holy Clarity: The Practice of Planning and Evaluation*[2] suggests, making sense is a sacred task, pleasing to God. Sacred tasks are not the property of any one person in any one role: they belong to all of us.

---

[2] Sarah Drummond, *Holy Clarity: The Practice of Planning and Evaluation* (Herndon, VA: Alban Institute, 2009).

Chapter 1 presents the theoretical framework of *Dynamic Discernment* and a theological reflection on it. In chapter 2, I write about the role of reason in change leadership. Reason is our God-given capacity to make sense of the world around us. It helps us to think analytically about complex situations, and it makes it possible for us to plan. The capacity to reason, and to lead others to reason, is a crucial leadership skill. Many from the business world who write about change rely on reason, organizing change into sequential steps through which a leader takes an organization, helping constituents to gain understanding. In this book, I describe reason-based change leadership as a "cognitive-developmental" approach. "Cognitive" in that it relates to seeing and understanding: making sense. "Developmental" in that an individual or community can grow in its capacity to make sense through the practice of teaching and learning.

In that chapter, I propose that the leadership role that corresponds most closely with a cognitive-developmental approach to change is that of the spiritual leader as teacher and planner. The leader helps the community to see a vision, a direction, and the steps needed to get there (a plan) by educating them regarding the need for change and change's requirements. Chapter 2 also describes some of the pitfalls of over-relying on reason. As Edwin Friedman writes, it is unreasonable to expect that those in our community are going to be reasonable. Emotions are often more powerful than reason, and they shape—and sometimes distort—our capacity to imagine. Power dynamics are almost always at work: the powerful person in a group can cause everyone to see that person's way without realizing that they have given over their own capacity to interpret. When made mindful that we have been drawn into another's perspective, we become defensive, sure that we are too reasonable for that to be true. The leader must be conversant in emotional systems and power dynamics in order to approach such situations with care. Quoting my colleague Amy McCreath, "Who cares that you're right?" Being right is only part of the story of leadership.

Chapter 3 explores the role of emotional systems in institutional change. Relying on Bowen's family systems theory and Friedman's expansion of that theory into the life of faith communities, I describe how interlocking triangles of relationships in community help us to make sense of change and inevitable resistance to it. Many religious leaders in the later twentieth century were inculcated in seminary and continuing education with the notion that emotional systems were all they needed to know about leadership. The good news is that a generation of faith leaders became aware of how congregations tended to do whatever it takes to maintain homeostasis, and they stopped blaming themselves for difficulties getting congregations unstuck. They learned to recognize triangulation and the ways in which those who rocked the boat for good reason could be unfairly scapegoated.

Conversely—and here is the bad news—a single-minded focus in ministerial leadership education on family systems theory also created a generation of leaders who saw communities as sets of interlocking triangles and nothing more. Considering that we live in a hyperrational world, it is understandable that exposure to a different way to make sense of communal behavior will bring about in us the zeal of the convert. All zeal fades with time, and we must be able to see from other perspectives as well.

The leadership practice associated with emotional systems that I propose in chapter 3 is that of self-differentiation. Friedman writes that in order to lead effectively in the midst of emotional triangles all around us, we must cultivate a separate-yet-together style of leadership, where we are whole ourselves and able to tell where we end and others begin. Whereas a cognitive-developmental approach calls upon the leader to explain, emotional systems call upon leaders to model self-possession and nonanxiety. Determining which situation calls for which leadership practice requires wisdom. Neither reason nor emotion alone takes into account the important and at times invisible role of power dynamics.

Chapter 4 attends to power. The most rational change leader (and the most well-differentiated to boot) still cannot function without savvy and strategy as relates to power. From the individual in a congregation who has and gives a lot of money to the former pastor who cannot help but chime in with opinions, power dynamics are critically important, and anyone who has served in religious leadership can share examples of times they have underestimated that importance and paid a price for their naïveté. The sources of power in communities of all kinds vary, and they are more complicated than meets the eye.

A member of a faith community could have more or less influence over the decisions of that organization depending on their wealth, health, family connections, professional status, duration of involvement, previous leadership roles, friends and allies, possession of information, attractiveness, and persuasiveness. None of those attributes necessarily means the Holy Spirit is more likely to speak through that person, and yet the person's capacity to get heard will vary with their power resources. In an attempt to be good and kind, religious leaders tend to overlook power dynamics where the source of power is an earthly one. By overlooking the role of power, leaders give away a key strategic tool that could help them to bring about transformation. By ignoring power dynamics, leaders allow the individuals with power to always win.

The leadership practice in chapter 4 emerges from two different sources of knowledge: liberation theology and critical path thinking. Liberation theology is a body of wisdom originating from the margins of society. Questions about life's meaning and purpose posed by those who have been decentered and disempowered generate different answers than the theologies that have had full audiences in the world of centered and empowered Christian scholarship over the centuries. Liberation theology fosters conscientization—an awakening of sorts—in their communities. Conscientization is not enough, however, for a community to experience transformation. Awake, the community recognizes the situation in which they find themselves, and then they must plot out a path through which grassroots energies find purchase with the powers that be, enabling meaningful change in the right places, connecting the goals of the historically oppressed with the motivations of those with more power. Critical path thinking includes organizing dimensions of a community's work into units, sequencing those units, and intentionally considering the top-down and bottom-up ways in which power can be used for the good. I call these shared goals "pockets of possibility" between those with top-down and bottom-up power, and leaders must be ready to help their communities identify those pockets. Instead of ignoring the role of power, critical path thinking conducts different sources of power so that they sing together in harmony.

Just as each chapter in this book provides one theoretical concept and a connected leadership practice, each chapter concludes with a fictional case study or workshop exercise. Cases are not drawn from any one particular "true" story, although several of them are amalgamations of numerous, different, real-life situations. The case studies help readers to consider how the dynamic in question—reason, emotion, or power—can be identified, connecting immediately to leadership practices for that dynamic. Workshop exercises at the conclusion of a chapter help the reader to consider how a leader might make sense of a situation using the frameworks of that chapter.

I believe in human capacity for change. That said, I am sober about change's potential on both communal and individual levels.

There are such things as points of no return, after which needed change is costlier than individuals or communities are willing to tolerate, and things fall apart. I believe that knowledge of change dynamics, enriched and critiqued by theology, provides leaders with something they need in this complicated point in human history. Change is changing faster than ever, and yet we need not allow ourselves or our communities to become overwhelmed. The church has survived and thrived through practices of adaptation. The adaptation we need today is capacity to lead change amidst complex communal dynamics.

A one-stop shop for change theories that each describes attributes of what happens in faith communities. A glossary of terms for those who care about change and want to help their communities to change for the good. A toolbox for leaders who know they need to adjust based on differing circumstances but do not know which tool helps in which situation. May you find all these resources and more as you continue to explore *Dynamic Discernment*.

.•1

How We Think about Change

A New Picture of How Communities Change

The theoretical framework upon which the arguments of this book hangs is shown in Figure 1.1.

The framework requires some immediate description, caveats, and clarifications, although each chapter will further define and justify it. The first thing a reader might note is that it is organized in a hierarchical fashion, with the realm of God at the top and the lived experience of incarnation at the bottom. The limitation of that design is obvious: God is not "up there," with us created beings "down here." God is everywhere, and also above us, not literally but in the form of God's dominion over us. To capture both an immanent (everywhere) and transcendent (reigning over us) God in a two-dimensional diagram is not possible; therefore, I privilege the transcendent and compensate with thoroughgoing descriptions of the immanent.

Second, a reader will note the use of the term "God's imagination for creation" used as a preferred alternative to what another might have named "God's will." Consider Augustine's City of God, where the fifth-century mystic-theologian imagined that coexisting with reality as we know it is a parallel universe where God's will is carried out. Of course, Augustine was not writing about quantum physics, but today's science fiction often surfaces a similar idea of a parallel universe that is overlaid on this life, not in a separate location, but in a separate realm.

Christians have interpreted Augustine over the years by using a politically flawed but not yet satisfactorily replaced term, the

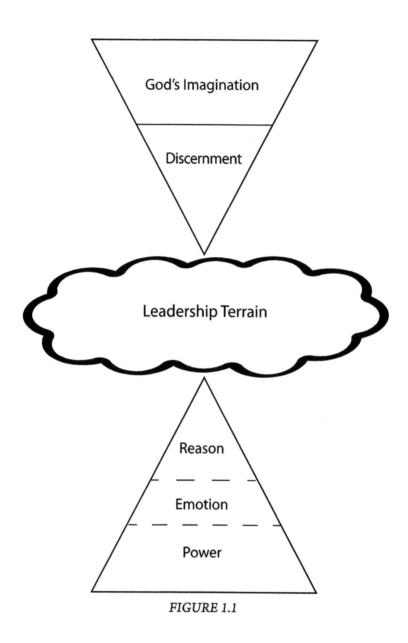

FIGURE 1.1

"kingdom of God." Some traditions, like the United Church of Christ, use the substitute language of a "kin-dom," which captures one dimension of God's imagination, where human beings treat one another like family. Although I believe that one attribute of the alternative universe of God's imagination for us includes this image of human beings loving each other like family, many attributes are lost in this reduction of kingdom language, which is, in the end, why I use the term "imagination" over "kingdom."

Theological or pastoral imagination, an idea developed most fully by Miroslav Volf and Dorothy Bass,[3] and explored by many practical theologians, provides a guide for the practice of ministry. Ministerial leaders consider, "What is the world as God imagines it? What is my role in making this realm look more like that one?" Imagination captures the transcendent nature of God, in that we recognize that God's imagination for our world is superior to anything a human being could ask or imagine. It also captures God's immanence or omnipresence, as we all have imaginations into which we can tap, and through our God-given creative minds we find a portal between our world and God's realm, kingdom, universe: whichever term we find least limiting.

The spiritual practice we use to find a connection with God's imagination for us as individuals, communities, and the whole of creation is "discernment." Discernment includes an array of cognitive and spiritual tasks: seeing, feeling, intuiting, interpreting, verbalizing, communicating. It is more than reading reality with our minds but also sensing it in every way a person can sense. Discernment relies heavily on the Holy Spirit, to which all have access by virtue of God's grace and our faith. Unlike the earthly terrain, where reason, emotion, and power shape and sometimes distort our perspectives, the realm of God's imagination and discernment

---

[3] Dorothy Bass and Miroslav Volf, "A Theological Understanding of Christian Practices," in *Practicing Theology: Beliefs and Practices in Christian Life*, 13–32 (Grand Rapids, MI: Eerdmans, 2002).

of it are equally available to all. God's imagination might be nebulous, but our discernment of God's will brings that imagination quite literally down to earth.

The Christian tradition teaches us that God's realm has not yet fully merged with creation. Jesus came to help us to find reconciliation between those worlds. He taught us the contours and rules of God's realm, which upended previous human interpretations of how we are supposed to live and how we are to treat each other. His death and resurrection were the ultimate in-breaking from the realm of God into creation, and we believe Jesus will come again. Will he come again in the form of perfect alignment between the realities of God's imagination and earthly existence, or will he descend in a chariot or on a cloud? We do not know. But in the intervening time, it is ours to connect, and reconnect, the disjuncture between God's imagined world and our own, which is striving toward God's imagination as an ultimate goal, which we ourselves cannot attain without God's grace.

The Space between Theology and the Practice of Leadership

The space between the earthly terrain and God's imagination is depicted in Figure 1.1 as the space in which leadership takes place. It is here where leaders have the opportunity to help communities connect with the practice of discernment, and thus the will of God. The theoretical framework depicts the leadership terrain as transcendent over the earthly plane but not quite in the realm of discernment and God's imagination, for leaders are human beings. As human beings, leaders must cultivate practices of rising above the fray, closer to the Holy Spirit rather than drawn—or sucked— into the dynamics this book seeks to aid in interpreting.

The leadership terrain is a space from which leaders draw on a variety of practices that originate from, and correspond to, different change dynamics. In chapters 2–4, three different dynamics that play out in communities will connect with three different bodies of leadership strategy that are most effective in the midst of those dynamics. To understand the repertoire of strategies, one must understand first the dynamics with which each practice connects.

The World in Which We Lead: Broken yet Beloved[4]

The lower portion of the theoretical framework corresponds with life on this earthly plane: incarnation, creation, the material, and the corporeal. Lower than God in a metaphysical sense, this diagram uses the physical lowness as a metaphor for the ways in which God reigns over us, and we find ourselves in what in Hebrew is called the *tohu wa-bohu*, a difficult-to-translate description of the conditions on earth before God said, "Let there be light."[5] In this primordial mix, we find the three different dynamics explored in this book, but of course, ultimately, so much more.

The three dynamics of reason, emotion, and power, are organized in descending fashion from the dynamic most receptive to leadership (reason) to the dynamic least receptive (power). Whereas reason is a level on which leaders and their constituents connect through practices of teaching and planning (see chapter 2), power hides from connection (see chapter 4) for the sake of its own self-preservation. Emotion (chapter 3) rests somewhere in between: sometimes leaders can harness emotion in community, and other times it behaves like an unbreakable horse.

Reason in the earthly plane, the lower portion of Figure 1.1, corresponds with making sense in the leadership terrain. Leaders can connect with a community's capacity to reason by teaching and

---

[4] I borrow the language of "broken yet beloved" from Sharon Thornton, *Broken yet Beloved* (St. Louis: Chalice Press, 2002).

[5] I was introduced to this idea by my colleague, Gregory Mobley, who used this Hebrew expression in a sermon at Andover Newton Theological School.

explaining and clarifying. Specifically as relates to change, leaders can help a community to understand why a change is needed, and what is the best way to achieve it, given all the alternatives. They connect sense-making with planning in order to point a community toward a new set of goals and realistic means for reaching those goals. Ministerial leaders can take advantage of well-trod avenues for sense-making communication, such as preaching, speaking, and writing about change. But reason is not enough, and, in fact, if it is the only tool a leader has in a toolbox, sense-making can become an unsturdy crutch, prone to breaking when leaned on too hard.

Emotion is different: it sometimes shapes reason, and at other times distorts it. Whereas a person who overrelies on reason might understand emotion to be a sensation experienced by an individual, in reality, emotion weaves through communities. Understanding how emotion works is immensely helpful to leaders trying to understand why a community is functioning the way it is, as well as understanding their own feelings and motivations. The leadership practice associated with emotion in this theoretical framework does not dive into the emotional system but rather cultivates practices of separate-yet-togetherness. Emotional systems respond best to leaders who are able to connect to the community without becoming enmeshed in it. This counterintuitive leadership practice can result in a leader not seeming to care, but the alternative is a leader who, in an unhealthy organization, goes down with the ship.

As previously stated, power is impervious to leadership. Where sense-making using reason is a skill in which leaders are trained through institutions of rational learning (college, graduate school), and emotional systems can be untangled when a leader is able to maintain a healthy understanding of where they end and other people begin, power preserves itself by its stealth. As I write this book, Donald Trump's presidency seems it could weather any poor choice on Trump's part. He impulsively throws out epithets that do not just offend but betray an inner life that is selfish and full of hate. Yet even on a question of whether he said the words he was reported to have said to a room full of elected leaders, those around him cannot agree whether he called Haiti, El Salvador, and the nations of Africa "shitholes." Why is a simple fact—the words from a president's mouth—subject to opinion at all? Because the economy is in good shape right now, which gives President Trump power: because those who have much want more. Because a person in a position of power will be protected at the cost of both reason and emotion.

Jesus came among us to upend flawed understandings about power. Where his listeners believed that power resulted from wealth, prestige, ancestry, and authority, Jesus said that, in God's imagination, the last shall be first. A baby is to become king. In this pre-parousia space on earth, Jesus's words are quickly forgotten, and those who have power quickly reassert the old rules when that power is under threat.

Chapter 4 will make two proposals regarding a leadership repertoire amidst power. First, power is like gravity: it is part of life and leadership. "Eradication" of power is simply impossible, and leaders must be able to work with and amidst power in order to be effective. It needs to take its rightful place at the table without sitting at its head. Undisciplined, power corrupts. Leading in the midst of power must coordinate grassroots (bottom-up) and authority-based (top-down) forces, using dialogue to traverse between those two loci of power in search of pockets of possibility for mutual benefit.

Second, power is inherently evasive. We find it easier to admit that we are reasonable and emotional than to admit we have power. Not because we are embarrassed, or even because we are naïve, but because pointing out our power where we have it might cause someone to try to take it away. Talking openly about power is particularly difficult in justice-seeking communities for obvious reasons: fighting misuse of power is sometimes the very mission of such organizations. Finding a vocabulary for discussing it is essential to prevent power from retreating underground, where it influences the community stealthily and thus unhealthily.

Our Assumptions about Human Will and Change

Change does not just happen.

Take a moment to meditate on those words, and then turn that phrase about like a cube with six facets (Figure 1.2).

1. Change does not just happen. It *results* from forces both evident and hidden beneath the surface.
2. Conversely, at the opposite side of the cube: change does not just happen, it is *caused*; the question is in what direction, how, and by whom?
3. Change does not just happen, but rather it *results from hard work*, inside and out, on the part of change agents.
4. Again, conversely: change does not just happen, in that *hard work is only a small part* of what meaningful change requires.
5. Change does not just happen, in the sense of *simple cause and effect*. It emerges from complexity and sets more complexity into motion.
6. That complexity is not to be confused with inevitability: change does not just happen, and *yet it can happen justly or unjustly* depending on the thoughtfulness of those leading it, or lack thereof.

Andover Newton President Emeritus Nick Carter kept a Rubik's Cube on his desk. For him, it served as a metaphor for what it was like to lead an institution in need of change, but where every change in one direction causes an opposite reaction, possibly in an undesirable direction. The Rubik's Cube serves as a reminder that change is replete with ironies and tensions. We can characterize

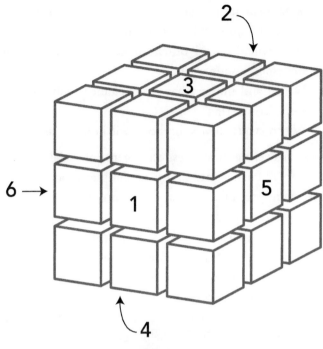

FIGURE 1.2

and define change in the abstract, but in lived experience all the different colors get mixed up. Even among those who lead change for a living, few take time to investigate their own assumptions about what change is and how it happens.

In the field of strategic philanthropy, organizations that give money to causes for the sake of social innovation are more and more commonly expecting change agents to articulate a "theory of change." In other words, those in the position of funding innovation want to be persuaded the social innovator has a logical, sound, and demonstrable case to make for why a series of actions—or inputs—will result in desired reactions—or impact. A theory of change answers the following questions:

1. Who are you seeking to influence or benefit (target population)?

2. What benefits are you seeking to achieve (results)?
3. When will you achieve them (time period)?
4. How will you and others make this happen (activities, strategies, resources, etc.)?
5. Where and under what circumstances will you do your work (context)?
6. Why do you believe your theory will bear out (assumptions)?[6]

Upon answering these questions, agents of social change organize a theory of change into simple or complex models so they can evaluate the impact of actions and continuously refine the theory of change based on evidence.

Yet the limitations of making philanthropic decisions based on an organization's stated theory of change leap to mind. Seminal author and thinker on theories of change, Paul Brest, writes that many organizations are not equipped to align their actions with their hoped-for impact before a funder has invested in their work. He recommends a developmental approach that helps an organization move from apparent effectiveness—anecdotally successful innovations—to proven effectiveness based on rigorous and data-driven evaluation.[7] Even Brest neglects in this calculation to consider the power dynamic that ensues when a funder insists on a beneficiary thinking in a particular way—their way—about inputs and impact. The order is a tall one.

The Gap between Beliefs and Actions

Social innovation scholar Michael Forti writes, "Simply putting boxes and lines down on paper doesn't guarantee that your organization will make better decisions."[8] Even the most reflective persons find

---

[6] Matthew Forti, "Six Theory of Change Pitfalls to Avoid," *Stanford Social Innovation Review*, May 23, 2012.

[7] Paul Brest, "The Power of Theories of Change," *Stanford Social Innovation Review*, Spring 2010.

[8] Forti, "Six Theory of Change Pitfalls to Avoid."

that careful investigation of their theories of change uncovers inconsistencies. The Apostle Paul writes, "I do not understand my own actions, for I do not do what I want, but I do the very thing I hate" (Romans 7:15). Is it not better, however, for organizations and individuals to at least think about their theories of change: the assumptions they make about what will result from the choices they make and the actions they take?

Within the individual decision-maker—namely, ourselves—we often discover that our behaviors do not match with what it is we say we want. And this is not just in the case of moral failings, but even in our most noble pursuits. Consider my own attitude toward ecology. I say to myself, "I believe that every person has a role to play in healing our planet's suffering environment." I do my best to turn off lights, recycle, travel in ways that rely on fossil fuels sparingly, and reuse what I might otherwise throw away.

Yet do I really believe that these efforts make the kind of difference that will be required? Would I not be better off using the same energy I expend on recycling advocating for change at the governmental level, or making more money I could give to environmental causes? No, when I truly think about it, I do not engage in ecological practices at home because I think it will heal the earth. I do so in order to live my life according to values: that which I seek to change is, first and foremost, myself. Even by investigating this one set of behaviors, I come to see that my assumptions about my motivation, and the impact for which I hope, are not what I initially thought when querying my own choices. If I were to consider every little choice I make, day in and day out, and challenge it as I have with the ecology question, I am quite sure I would find as many disconnections as connections between my actions and my hoped-for impact on the world around me.

In communities, these inconsistencies and complexities increase exponentially, as many different, thoughtful people have very different ideas about the relationship between cause and effect. Consider the example of leaders in churches where attendance is in decline. Two leaders might have divergent opinions about why people come to church, what they are looking for, and what it would take to increase attendance. If those two people dive into problem-solving unhesitatingly, they may later be surprised when they come into conflict. Yes, Forti is correct that putting boxes and lines on paper is not enough for organizations to become more effective. But in order to even think about impact, some discussion on the relationship between actions and reactions is important as organizations become more diverse and complex.

Robert Kegan and Lisa Lahey's *Immunity to Change: How to Overcome It and Unlock the Potential in Yourself and Your Organization*[9] examines adult development and its impact upon capacity for change. For more than thirty years, Kegan in particular has sought to debunk the notion that the human mind stops developing when the human body stops growing. Even though our brains might not get "taller" after we stop growing, our cognitive functions can become more complex and able to manage irony, contradiction, multiple perspectives, and coexisting truths. Or not. The "or not" corresponds with our "immunity to change," the competing commitments that prevent us from making changes in our lives we purport to want. Kegan and Lahey use a three-column diagram to demonstrate how this immunity counterweights desire for change. Table 1.1 imagines the immunity to change, for example, of a person who wishes to stop smoking.

Kegan and Lahey argue that individuals and organizations get stuck when they focus only on the middle column and insist on a behavioral change. Failure to recognize the competing commitment—what causes us to hold onto harmful behavior—ensures that change will elude us. The developmental task surfaces

---

[9] Robert Kegan and Lisa Laskow Lahey, *Immunity to Change: How to Overcome It and Unlock the Potential in Yourself and Your Organization* (Boston: Harvard University Press, 2009).

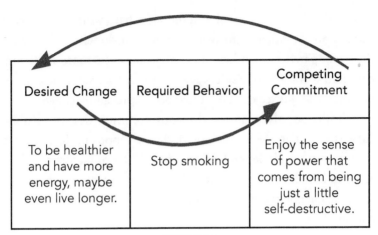

Desired Change	Required Behavior	Competing Commitment
To be healthier and have more energy, maybe even live longer.	Stop smoking	Enjoy the sense of power that comes from being just a little self-destructive.

TABLE 1.1

when immunity to change prevents our development. Immunity to change is a helpful framework for describing a theory of change. We say we want to do this, but then we do not. Taking that extra reflective step yields more satisfying results. The smoker wishing to quit must examine their reasons for enjoying a bit of self-destructiveness and find a way to think differently about those impulses if they are to meet their espoused goal.

Kegan and Lahey's theory drastically overestimates the power of insight. It underestimates the hold that emotions can exert on our capacity to reason. Furthermore, it assumes a certain amount of power over one's circumstances that does not prove realistic among most people. That said, the more we can do to put language to theories of change, the more we can do to uncover our sometimes faulty assumptions, assumptions that may run counter to our most cherished beliefs.

Reason Is Pleasing; Change Is Messy

We return now to the image of a Rubik's Cube. Earlier, I wrote about the opposing sides of the cube. On the one side, change emerges;

on the other side, it is caused. On one side, hard work is what really matters; on the other, hard work has little to do with effectiveness when compared with other forces that are even more influential than hard work. On one side, cause and effect are value-neutral; on the other side, justice can be—must be—a prevailing concern.

Within ourselves, and within our communities, the Rubik's Cube is in a state of multicolored chaos. Opposing forces are at work within us all, depending on a multitude of factors that have led us to be who we are and to think how we think. By that logic, no single change theory can capture all that goes into the transformation of a person or a community, an institution or a nation. Capacity to name the complexity and function within it—planning, guiding, and anchoring change—is the new leadership challenge of the twenty-first century.

Articulating a theory of change is a good place to start for a person or organization who wants to work more thoughtfully and effectively. Forti's questions guide discernment of a theory of change: identification of the target population, hoped-for results, time period in which work will take place, activities and other inputs that will lead to results, setting in which results will take place, and assumptions about why the named activities are the right ones to lead to the hoped-for results. Some might say that the last step regarding assumptions—"Why do you believe your theory will bear out (assumptions)?"—is actually the heart of a theory of change.

Forti goes on to name pitfalls in developing a theory of change, and two among them speak to the "why" question about assumptions. He writes that organizations' leaders at times fail to confirm the plausibility of their assumptions about how change happens. He notes that organizations that take nothing for granted as relates to the connection between inputs and impact, but rather study the space between actions and consequences, are more likely to succeed. I can think of many examples of organizations that built a whole initiative on a faulty—implausible—theory of change. Yet I can think of few instances where the leaders behind those initiatives stopped and asked themselves, "I've been assuming that if I do *this*, then *that* would happen; what if I was wrong?" Forti also names as a pitfall the failure to take their contexts into account. What we do, and the results of our actions, have a great deal to do with factors beyond our control. If we do not understand external factors, we fail to respect their power to influence the results of our actions.

I have written elsewhere about the connection between "conditions" and "interventions" (Figure 1.3). Conditions describe situations in need of change. Interventions are programmatic plans for action. A disconnection between the condition in need of transformation and the intervention leaders' plan means a problem with the leaders' theory of change. "If I do *this*, then *that* will happen" may be a sentence that is simply illogical, depending on "this" and "that." What is our desired outcome, and what is the action that will most likely lead to it? The time we dedicate to that question, and the time we do not dedicate, say a great deal about what kind of leader we are or want to be.

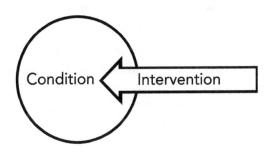

FIGURE 1.3

Possibilities over Problems

Thinking and talking about problems is draining, depressing, and the opposite of fun. Conditions are, more often than not, problems; otherwise they would not come to the attention of leaders in communities. But hyperfocus on problems is itself a sign and source of institutional dysfunction. In his book *Community: The Structure of Belonging*,[10] Peter Block writes that focus on problems over possibilities is one of the main obstacles to communal imagination.

Ironically, Block's argument that institutions focus too much on problems and not enough on possibilities points back to the idea that some leaders have unhealthy theories of change. I take my own experience in theological education as an example. For nearly thirteen years, I have served a seminary that ardently sought a sustainable path. Enrollment was going down. Buildings were falling apart. Donors were distracted by other philanthropic opportunities and worried about giving to an organization that did not have a financially viable long-term plan. Amidst those herculean obstacles, I convinced myself that if I worked harder—that if all of us did—all these problems could be fixed. I had no choice but to embrace this faulty theory of change in order to keep on going until we—the administration, faculty, and board—could see another path forward. The possibility that hard work was not the answer was too awful to consider, yet in retrospect I wonder if I could have been kinder to myself by facing the disconnect between hard work and desired results.

Focus on problems need not be draining if an organization has a theory of change that is healthy: realistic, optimistic, and compassionate to self and others.

1. Realistic: One can make a logical connection between the actions proposed and the condition in need of change.
2. Optimistic: The connective space between interventions and conditions is illuminated by hope and gives goodness the benefit of the doubt.
3. Compassionate: The intervention and its related condition are part of creation, which is inherently good in God's eyes; we must treat it that way.

---

[10] Peter Block, *Community: The Structure of Belonging* (San Francisco: Berrett-Koehler, 2008).

With these three guiding attitudes at work, an organization is ready to think about problems. Not exclusively or obsessively, of course, which is Block's concern, but not as an afterthought either. How will a good intervention, meant to bring about change, even be evaluated after the fact without a sense of what the intervention was seeking to transform in the first place? Elsewhere,[11] I have used the condition/intervention diagram as a model for planning an evaluation. I have argued that leaders usually do better at evaluating *interventions*—were they enjoyable? well-attended? fun?—than they are at evaluating changes in a *condition*. In other words, we are better at talking about what has happened than we are at considering what has changed, or not changed, as a result. So if transformation was the whole point of our actions, we are missing more than half the story when we focus on the interventions rather than the conditions to which they were meant to attend.

What is the connection between theology and a theory of change? Can we go so far as to understand theology as a theory of change in itself? In his book *Believing, Caring, and Doing in the United Church of Christ*, an introduction to theology from a UCC point of view, Gabriel Fackre writes that we construct theology using the following lenses: the gospel, scripture, our tradition, and the experience of today's generation. I have taught students that we can imagine these four perspectives as four nested circles in a telescope (see Figure 1.4), and we can point that telescope at any situation with the intention of making sense of it theologically. Fackre writes that when the UCC loses track of its sources of theology, we forget who we are.[12] In his honor, therefore, I turn now to a theological perspective on theories of change.

Those whose faith is rooted in a trinitarian understanding of God already engage the practice of communicating with one another

---

[11] Drummond, *Holy Clarity.*

[12] Gabriel Fackre, *Believeing, Caring, and Doing in the United Church of Christ* (Cleveland: United Church Press, 2005).

using a shared vocabulary for that which is abstract and ephemeral. Trinitarians understand the nature of God in three persons: Father, Son, and Holy Ghost in the most traditional language. Thus what cannot be described perfectly except by God herself can be described

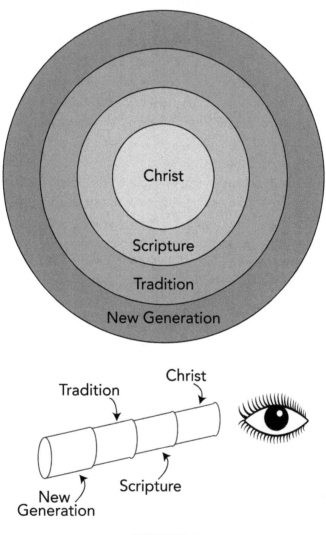

FIGURE 1.4

more adequately by breaking its un-understandable nature down into more manageable parts. Consider the meditation that follows here on the nature of the Trinity, which will give way to a description of how this book will break that which is difficult to face head-on—change leadership—into different perspectives, thus rendering change more approachable and given to exploration.

God is our creator and point of origin, and God is to whom we believe we will return after this earthly existence is complete. God is powerful over us, corrects us when we are wrong, and nurtures us toward that which is right. As these qualities resemble the best of strong parents, we call God "father" in one of God's attributes. God is not a man; God as father is a metaphor, and a good—yet imperfect—one at that. And father is only part of the story.

For God is also One who came among us in Jesus, and Jesus is our friend. Jesus talked to us in words we could understand, describing God's loving nature, and hopes for humanity and all of creation. Jesus was put to death by his own people's leaders, with their complicity and consent. He then overcame death and rose again, thus establishing God's might in a whole new way: God has dominion even over death itself. In these ways, we at times refer to Jesus as our redeemer, who bailed us out of a metaphorical jailhouse, where life lacked meaning beyond mere survival. This redemption freed us to live for God, loving each other and making the world a better place; this redemption gave our lives meaning. And yet God, not only a father, is not only a friend and liberator either.

God is also an energy, diffuse and invisible but omnipresent and able to penetrate even what seem to be the most God-forsaken situations on earth. The Holy Spirit, sent among the disciples as a guiding sensibility in dramatic fashion at Pentecost, is what we feel guiding "our" choices for what we want to see happen in our lives, and the events that happen to us. When we declare in worship, "Come Holy Spirit! Come!" we humbly acknowledge that the Holy

Spirit was with us all along, but sometimes our attentions were directed elsewhere. Sometimes we were overrelying on ourselves and thinking we could handle our lives without God's guidance and assistance. The Holy Spirit does not discipline us through abandoning us; it is upon us the moment we call its name.

How are the ideas presented in this book similar to the theology of the Trinity? Perhaps to even make the comparison is heresy of sorts, yet the Trinity inspires me to take that which is overwhelming and break it down into manageable parts that are easier for me to understand. In this book, I will present an argument that communities that have come together toward a common cause are complicated entities. "Complicated" does not mean "impenetrable." It simply means that communities are more than meets the eye.

Leaders will avert their eyes if they are too overwhelmed to even look at the dynamics at work in the settings they serve. Just as looking at the sun directly can cause injury and we need instruments in order to do it safely. We need to face the chronically unreasonable, emotionally fused, and power-obsessed with special care. For we love our communities, and we need to keep on loving them if we are, as leaders, to be of any use to them. Varied perspectives render analysis more manageable and make possible forgiveness and acceptance of human flaws. When we understand not just where individuals are coming from, but also how dynamics form and shape human behaviors, we are more generous with those who are resistant to our leadership. We seek understanding more than opportunities to lay blame. We also see more than we can with the dismissive naked eye, which looks past that which is difficult to fathom.

This book's theoretical framework finds connections in the Trinity's God-in-three-persons. First, God is a God of transcendent power. Power is the most elusive of the dynamics that take place in communities. No one who has it wants to admit it, especially when such an admission might draw attention to power, with the result of someone wanting to take it away. One could make an argument that only God has power not susceptible to corruption. Humans can lord their power over others or use their power to cause their communities to reflect God's work in the world, shaping and correcting human communities. Those with power are subject to corruption, and they are also necessary to make God's vision a reality.

Second, Jesus came among us not just as a liberator from death but also as a teacher of a new form of reason. His messages disrupted previously held assumptions, formal religious teachings, and the conventional knowledge of the time. He was known among his followers as their teacher, and teachers provide new understandings. From new understanding, changes in behavior are bound to follow. The form of reason this book promotes is specific: it is reason guided by Jesus's teachings and the upended power structures of the gospel. Jesus healed the bodies of those whose lives he touched. He also healed the defects in their reasoning through teaching them. Jesus's healing restores individuals to communities and restores communities to health and wholeness.

Third, the Holy Spirit makes itself known in communities through emotions. We do not see, touch, hear, smell, or taste the Holy Spirit; we know it through an elusive but ineffably real sixth sense. We feel the Holy Spirit in and around us, but the word "feel" does not mean palpable. Just as emotion has a hold on us that motivates us and moves us to action without basis in that which makes rational sense, the Holy Spirit is a presence we feel and deeply know. Because emotion is difficult to describe and cannot be perceived with one among the physical five senses, we sometimes think it can be ignored, or manipulated, or instructed to go away.

Yet much like the Holy Spirit, emotion is not going anywhere. Jesuit spiritual directors teach their directees to listen to their emotions, with the understanding that God, through the Holy Spirit, is trying to tell them something. To do so requires an emotional self-regulation that can detect the difference between that which we feel and the assumed feelings of those around us. That level of self-awareness is difficult, but not impossible to sustain. The trinitarian Christian perspectives on change can be an overarching set of truths guiding change leadership in Christian communities, but just because they are overarching does not mean they need not be articulated. In fact, in faith communities, frequent reminders of the connection between the life of the community and theology is perhaps the most important function for the faith community leader. Even the most thoroughly catechized Christian needs reminders that we are, in faith communities, part of a drama much bigger than ourselves. Knowledge that there is an overarching truth to that which we face is both humbling and comforting, especially on the days when we wonder why we must face the challenges, and not just the joys, of living in faith and in community.

The purpose of calling out three different dynamics of change is to help the ministerial leader to understand what is happening in people and communities more fully, and to respond accordingly, thus becoming more effective in their leadership. The capacity to see from all three of these angles is a leadership art. I studied pastoral care under Professor Katherine Clark of Weston Jesuit Theological Seminary in the 1990s, and to hear her describe the nature of pastoral care, the sole purposes of a pastor's intervention is to understand and to demonstrate understanding. When the minister expresses understanding of the thoughts, feelings, and sufferings of a person—even if those thoughts, feelings, and sufferings are remote from the minister's experience—healing happens. Twenty-one years after taking her course, I still think of Professor Clark when I hear those words, "You get it!" That exclamation, to a pastoral leader, is the highest praise.

If those to whom we minister and those we lead do not feel like we understand them, we cannot do our pastoral work. Feeling understood is the beginning of trust. If we ascribe to all those to whom we minister a single set of motivations, we simply cannot understand them, as there is no one way in which people make sense of the world. Therefore, this book provides three different perspectives, not because there are precisely three, but by way of saying that there is not one but many forces at work in communities of people. Imposing just one way of making sense of the world disrespects the complexity of the lives of those whom we serve. Colleague the Rev. Amy McCreath advises clergy, "Congregations are not problems to be solved." When we bring a single lens to their dynamics, we reduce them. Therefore, we take up three lenses as a means of honoring the multiple layers just under the surface of persons' behaviors and the ways in which they function in community.

Exercise: Theory-of-change Evaluation

When we think together about our theory of change ("We do *this*, and *that* happens") in a faith community or religious organization, we cannot overrely on unspoken assumptions to articulate our theological worldview. People of faith need to constantly remind themselves what our theology has to say about how we should live our lives, individually and communally. We are forgetful by nature, and we also live in a diverse and complex society where numerous different worldviews shape the assumptions of those around us. To think theologically is to think counterculturally, and thinking counterculturally requires discipline.

Therefore, this exercise (Table 1.2) marries theory-of-change evaluation questions described earlier in this chapter with a Christian worldview. The discipline suggested is to think theologically first and foremost, before even attempting to answer the question. Theology and assumptions are not the same. Theology cannot remain unspoken when discernment is underway.

Theory-of-change question	What is God calling you to do?	What do Jesus' teachings tell us? What are the resurrection implications?	Where do we feel the Holy Spirit guiding us, and through whom is she speaking?	Therefore . . .
Whom are you seeking to influence or benefit (target population)?				
What benefits are you seeking to achieve?				
When will you achieve them? (time period)				
How will you and others make this happen (activities, strategies, resources, etc.				
Where and under what circumstances will you do your work (context)?				
Why do you believe your theory will bear out?				

TABLE 1.2

Exercise: How We Are Different

The purpose of this exercise is for people to get to know their own assumptions better, either for themselves or in a group. It can help them see plainly how differently each of us thinks about change. In the case of using it in a gathering, the facilitator instructs the group:

Look at these six assertions about how change happens.

1. Change does not just happen, in that it comes as a result from forces both evident and hidden beneath the surface.
2. Conversely, at the opposite side of the cube: change does not just happen, it is made to happen; the question is in what direction, how, and by whom.
3. Change does not just happen, but rather it results from hard work, inside and out, on the part of change agents.
4. Again, conversely: change does not just happen, in that hard work is only a small part of what meaningful change requires.
5. Change does not just happen, in the sense of simple cause and effect. It emerges from complexity and sets more complexity into motion.
6. That complexity is not to be confused with inevitability: change does not just happen, and yet it can happen justly or unjustly depending on the thoughtfulness of those leading it, or lack thereof.

You will see that polar-opposite attitudes about change are grouped into twos: one and two, three and four, five and six. Read the list and ask yourself which of the two speaks to you; with which one would you tend to agree more readily? Circle it. When you are finished, turn to a neighbor and compare notes. Where did you circle the same predisposition, and where did you circle different ones? Where there are discrepancies, talk about your thinking, using examples from your life experiences.

.●2

Reason

The Role of Reason in Change Leadership

Early Christians formed their communities in contexts where reason was the ideal toward which the cultural elites strived. Greek ideals of the life of the mind ran alongside Christian teachings of a life of embodied faith.[13] The two—faith and reason—have lived side by side uncomfortably since those earliest days. Occasionally, conflict emerges, and times of change are the most likely moments in the life of a community when all tensions rise to the surface. Leaders must have a healthy relationship with reason in times of change, for it provides some of the most important tools for guiding a community through a time of change.

Although the tools to be described in this chapter—like lists we use in planning and lenses we use for analysis—might seem practical to the point of simplistic, seasoned leaders know that reason is one of the first human gifts to fly out the door when a community is anxious about change. Therefore, the leader must have those simple tools ready to share when others have lost track of that which makes sense.

A More Sufficient Equilibrium

In her study of the teaching methods of change guru Ronald Heifetz, Sharon Daloz Parks provides her interpretation of Heifetz's definition of the leader's role in communal change: the leader moves a community from an insufficient equilibrium, through

---

13 Parker Palmer, *The Active Life: A Spirituality of Work, Creativity, and Caring* (San Francisco: Jossey-Bass, 1999).

disequilibrium, to a more sufficient equilibrium.[14] This definition is one I trotted out as recently as yesterday morning, when I was having breakfast with a colleague who has been called to serve as president and dean of a seminary that is in need of a new equilibrium.

The definition Daloz Parks provides makes the role of leadership feel manageable. The definition honors that disequilibrium is a necessary part of the process, not to be avoided nor pathologized. It avoids language of "success" and "excellence" by presenting a realistic goal: a more sufficient equilibrium. Like many cognitive-developmental approaches to change leadership, these frameworks are useful insofar as they give a leader something upon which they can focus, rather than throwing up their hands, not knowing where to start.

A Cognitive-Developmental Approach

For the purposes of this chapter, the term "cognitive-developmental" is used to describe the approaches to change that correspond with communal reasoning. Let us return to the theoretical framework described in Figure 1.1. You can see in the image that reason rests at the top of the triangle signifying a human (earthly, fallen) community.

The location of reason in the framework is not accidental. Reason is located closer to the leadership terrain because it is the easiest dynamic to engage. A reasonable leader can connect with reasonable constituents by constructing plans, being sensible, and framing reality. Reason is but one dynamic, of course, for even the most reasonable people are not that way all the time. But a leader must reason well if they are to preserve their energy for the more difficult and draining dynamics of emotion and power.

So how do leaders interpret change in their communities using reason, and how do they connect with reasoning dynamics in the

---

[14] Sharon Daloz Parks, *Leadership Can Be Taught: A Bold Approach for a Complex World* (Boston: Harvard Business School Press, 2005).

community? A cognitive-developmental approach suggests that leaders do so using recognizing (i.e., cognition), and then they teach and plan the community toward a new vision (development). Leaders plan and explain, and explain and plan some more. They draw communities into a process of change that involves not just making lists, but helping others to see a new way. This is a process of building a new reality together.

Recognition

First, recognition: a key role for leaders is metaphorically seeing the community through a lens of love. Gene Outka writes in his classic tome on Christian ethics, *Agape: An Ethical Analysis*, that the heart of ethics is loving with equal regard.[15] I heard the advice from experienced pastor Heather Kirk-Davidoff to aspiring ministers that their first three years must be dedicated to serving congregations as their "historian-lovers." Scott Cormode writes in *Making Spiritual Sense: Christian Leaders as Spiritual Interpreters* that the role of the minister is to describe reality theologically, trusting that doing so plants seeds within the community that grow into a newly gospel-aligned way of being.[16] All three of these thinkers—a Christian ethicist, a pastor, and a religious leadership scholar—provide different ways of describing the same thing: a primary role of leaders is to regard their communities with honesty while holding the community in love.

I recently received a phone call from a colleague who was overjoyed about the results of a congregational retreat where I had played a role, and she wanted to thank me. I had spent time with leaders in a church that had attempted to combine forces with another faith community in town, only to have the deal fall

---

[15] Gene Outka, *Agape: An Ethical Analysis* (New Haven, CT: Yale University Press, 1972).

[16] Scott Cormode, *Making Spiritual Sense: Christian Leaders as Spiritual Interpreters* (Nashville: Abingdon Press, 2006).

apart at the last minute, as is so often the case. I said many things to the leaders in the church, but what seemed to penetrate most was when I offered *observations*, describing what I was hearing and seeing as they shared their story, six months after the events that brought partnership talks to a close.

I observed aloud that the members of the congregation seemed to really love each other and want to work together for the future. I noted that wounds seemed to remain, and that they might have work to do in forgiving those who were on the other side of the debate regarding the institution's preferred future. I noted that it seemed to me that both sides wanted the same thing: a healthy church. Those who wanted the union to take place had worked tirelessly, and I thanked them for it. Those who raised objections tried to do so transparently; they did so out of genuine concern, and I praised their courage for speaking up when feeling called to do so.

One could call my descriptions of what I saw an exercise in stating the obvious. Yet the results were rapid and astonishing: the pastor told me that some who had not been speaking to each other immediately embraced, forgave each other, and covenanted to rebuild their friendship. The pastor had tilled and toiled over soil, making it possible for me to toss in some seeds of observations for all to hear. Seeing the truth, and saying the truth, is a powerful act of leadership.

A word here about the role of consultants in institutional leadership, for it is in the realm of reason where they can be most useful. My father once told me, when I had been hired to consult for the first time, "Consultants steal your watch and then tell you what time it is." He did not mean this aphorism as a compliment, but over the years I have come to find it reassuring. Consultants can help a stuck organization to understand the time, simply by observing and describing the realities they perceive.

Yet there is no substitute for an executive leader who is ready to work to understand more clearly the realities facing the community and helping others to do the same. Consultants can help a setting whose leader is aware of the importance of accurately assessing and convincingly describing reality. The consultant can help to gather data and make sense of it, bringing and sharing an outsider's perspective. But reason-rooted leadership practice cannot be outsourced to consultants, only enhanced by them.

Recognizing and Visioning

So far, we have considered the role of the leader in communal cognition: grasping reality through theological lenses and describing that reality to a wider community. The leadership practice—the verb—associated with this work is "to vision," or "visioning." I have written elsewhere[17] and for years taught my students in leadership courses the following: change processes need not be utterly inclusive, every step of the way. Sometimes if they are, processes stall under the pressure of micromanagement. The only portion of a change initiative that absolutely must include everyone is visioning. In the visioning period of a change initiative, the leader provides settings for constituents to dream of a new reality. Not everyone will agree on a new reality, but if the leader alone brings the vision, that vision will not make it far.

In Christian scripture, visions begin as the property of the prophets. God expresses vision in a new way through Jesus's resurrecting love, transforming vision into a gift of the Holy Spirit. The prophets and the Holy Spirit function similarly as instruments communicating God's vision: God wants to give creation a word of wisdom, and God often chooses the least likely candidates for sharing that word. Any member of a community can be a vessel into whom God pours the vision for all. Therefore, inclusive

---

17 Drummond, *Holy Clarity*.

processes of visioning are essential in order to ensure that God's voice is not prevented access to a platform.

Consider the following workshop exercise I call the Polaroid Picture exercise, which is useful in large groups at an early phase in a change initiative. Playful and intimate, the exercise encourages those with different backgrounds and levels of leadership power and experience to vision together. Ask the group to get comfortable and then close their eyes.

"Picture this community fully alive," says the facilitator, who goes on to say, "Imagine what this setting looks like in God's imagination when it has realized its full potential. Take your time. Consider the sights, smells, and sounds you might encounter in that fully alive reality. Now, pretend you have a Polaroid camera. Take a picture of what you see. Shake the picture to get the vibrant colors to come out. When it seems like it has come into full resolution, open your eyes, turn to your neighbor, and show them your picture. Describe what it is you saw, and compare and contrast your imaginations for this community."

The role of the leader is to help the group to shape a coherent composite picture from a large number of different pictures. When a community comes to clarity and consensus around a mental picture for the future, there is little the group will be unwilling to try, or even unwilling to change, to make that picture a reality. I experienced an exercise where I was part of a group of faculty members and administrators from my school, on retreat and thinking together about the education we want to provide our students. The facilitator[18] had each of us write out six different notecards with our priorities for our program. She then instructed us to team up with another person and together choose the six that we considered most important; each pair had to keep six and lose six, which was not too hard because of similarities we found. Then, groups

---

[18] I thank Jeanne Peloso of Yale Divinity School for this exercise.

of two combined with other groups of two and again reduced to six priorities. Finally, the entire faculty and administration came together and reduced to six. This exercise was just one of many ways to create a group list of priorities.

Expecting a community to change in the absence of shared priorities or a composite picture borders on theft. Why would we take something away from a community, if not for the purpose of giving it something better? But get to that shared vision, and there is little else in a change process that needs to include everyone. Once the vision is cast, it is time to get down to the brass tacks of carrying it out, checking in with the community every step of the way, with that vision in hand and in mind.

Why are vision exercises important for a community, and what do they have to do with reason? One might consider the act of imagination to be far from reason, and rather in the ethereal realm of creativity. On the contrary, visioning has everything to do with a community making spiritual sense[19] of their purpose and the transformation the community seeks to bring about in the world. The exercise takes into account the way people envision reality—human reality and God's—differently from one another. It also suggests that aggregating a shared vision is an important first step in a change process. The exercise assumes that people are capable of engaging together in a pursuit: *We* want this, and therefore *we* need to do that. Perhaps not everybody will get their way, but everyone had a chance to add their voices. Referring back to the first chapter, the exercise is built on the assumption that people operate from a reasonable theory of change.

Some scholars believe that spiritual seeing and describing is the primary role of the leader, and that as the leader articulates reality—sees on behalf of the community—the wheels are set into motion. Others claim that visioning is merely a first step in a more

---

[19] Cormode, *Making Spiritual Sense*.

complex and methodical process. This transition from visioning to planning is where the term "developmental" comes into this chapter on cognitive-developmental approaches to change leadership. It is after a composite vision is cast, and the community has understood and perhaps even bought into it, that we move from lenses to lists.

Cognitive-developmental approaches to change leadership connect with a community's desire that leadership decisions make sense. Perhaps the highest compliment one can pay to an institutional change is, "That makes sense," and we credit the leader with that accomplishment. To-do lists are perhaps the ultimate artifact of the sense-maker. The lists presented by those who think and write about change from a cognitive-developmental point of view correspond to the stages through which a leader must bring a community so that change can be effective and sustainable. Consider this seminal list of stages of change from Harvard Business School's John Kotter:

1. establishing a sense of urgency;
2. creating the guiding coalition;
3. developing a vision and strategy;
4. communicating the change vision;
5. empowering broad-based action;
6. generating short-term wins;
7. consolidating gains and producing more change;
8. anchoring new approaches in the culture.[20]

Kotter's work, which originates from the business world but has been adapted across fields, makes certain claims about how change happens in organizations. Basing his findings on many years of consulting and research, Kotter suggests that there are certain stages through which a leader must bring an organization. Those stages build

---

[20] John P. Kotter, *Leading Change* (Boston: Harvard Business School Press, 1996), 21.

on one another, and yet they do not always happen in sequence. Kotter's step-by-step theory resembles other theories of change, or "stage theories," where steps sometimes shift in sequence and other times blend together. He writes in *Leading Change* about common mistakes that correspond to each stage, and how to avoid those mistakes.

1. Establishing a sense of urgency. In faith communities, the kinds of urgency to which leaders must respond looks less like market realities and more like cultural ones. Faith communities respond to injustice with a sense of urgency to overcome evil with good. Some faith communities additionally face urgent situations related to their own survival. Where religious organizations at one time needed to consider change as a matter of relevance and best practice, in my tradition and region, changing is the alternative to oblivion. The day before writing this chapter, I heard from a staff member at a church that is going through a period of discernment over their sustainability. The biggest area of contention among congregants is how truly urgent their financial situation is, and whether those in leadership are perhaps exaggerating how dire their straits really are. You can bet on it: the leaders are right, but would it not be so much more convenient if they were wrong?

In *Leadership without Easy Answers*,[21] Ronald Heifetz writes about giving communities change at a rate they can stand. To moderate the urgency in a community without letting it descend into anxiety—and thus panic and gridlock—is a leadership art in need of careful cultivation. In a post-2008 world, no organization is too big, too historic, or too prestigious to fail. The market crash that brought down Wall Street giants left many stunned, but we have had time to get past the shock and into a new reality. Sometimes facing the truth that none of our institutions is invincible is simply too awful for us. Much like adolescents who feel immortal

---

[21] Ronald A. Heifetz, *Leadership without Easy Answers* (Cambridge, MA: Harvard University Press, 1994).

but are shaken awake by near-death experiences, institutions are scared straight on their journeys to maturity. Maturity includes a sense of urgency that acknowledges that institutions are like any other kind of body, and bodies neither last forever nor can they survive every illness or injury inflicted upon them.

2. Creating the guiding coalition. One special dimension of faith communities, and one worthy of preservation, is that those in leadership in Christian organizations might not necessarily have great power in other parts of society. For instance, consider the head deacon who wears a three-piece suit to church and comports himself as though he were mayor, where during the week he serves as a school custodian. Consider the bank teller who spends the week taking orders and then is asked to chair the search committee for a new pastor. In God's realm, there is no distinction between those with societal power and without it. Yet faith communities need leaders who can be effective based on their God-given gifts, and the tension between empowering everyone and selecting just some can be difficult to reconcile.

Kotter writes, "Putting together a group with enough power to lead the change" and "getting the group to work together like a team" are crucial steps in leading change. Religious leaders have to take care to read power dynamics in their communities before pulling a team together. How can we balance the gospel's demand that the first shall be last with the necessity of pulling together a team that can make change happen? Again, this balancing act is more art than skill.

3. Developing a vision and strategy. The Polaroid Picture exercise has its obvious limitations. Recently, when I conducted that exercise with a group of seminary students beginning a new class with me, reactions ranged from puzzlement to downright humorlessness. I asked the students to picture our course fully alive, with them getting what they most need out of it. One said she could drum up a mental picture right away, and it was a picture of the only course she took last semester and enjoyed; this depressing overture felt something like a threat. Another said that he had a hard time picturing the class with him in it fully alive, because he kept envisioning himself looking goofy. I stressed to the students, and stressed again, that we need to construct vision together, which means honestly claiming the portion of a vision that is ours and that we wish to contribute, taking responsibility for our part in making the vision a reality.

A key difference between faith communities and other institutions is that we do not seek in our visioning process to come up with a picture only of what it is we want as individuals or even as a community. Instead, we seek to uncover God's vision, God's imagination, and God's will. No one person has unique access to God's imagination, so under the guidance of the Holy Spirit, we have to work together to create a cohesive composite picture based on our individual and communal interpretation.

A key similarity between faith communities and organizations with different goals is that both must move from visioning to strategy. Some faith communities believe themselves to be an exception to that rule, and they do so at their peril. As soon as we have crafted a vision for our communities, we must become obsessed with how to get from where we are to where we need to be. When we hear that obsessing over details is unfaithful, and that we should trust God more and plan less, we should be highly skeptical.

I have a colleague who consults with churches on leadership issues, particularly strategic planning. She told me a story of one church that put together a clear and coherent vision, and then the leaders mapped out a plan for how they would make that vision a reality. At the same time, she worked with another church that finished the visioning process and waited for the picture to emerge on its own. The latter church claims she did not do a good job as their consultant, and the former recommends her to anyone who will listen. This example teaches us that poor follow-through on strategy guarantees that even the most compelling vision will fail, whether the organization listens to the voice of the Holy Spirit or to the pressures of the market economy.

4. Communicating the change vision. Religious leaders are fortunate to have more opportunities to communicate change visions than might be the case in a company or school. With weekly public gatherings—namely, worship—and relationships rooted in conversation, religious leaders are communicators by trade. Some ministers believe that preaching on change visions for their communities violates the purpose of preaching, and in many cases, they are right in thinking that preaching about change initiatives misuses the power of the pulpit. And yet preaching in such a way that promotes a positive attitude toward transformation can till the soil on which leaders throw new seeds.

Religious leaders hesitate to instruct one another on how to comport themselves. Other types of institutions struggle with the same. In a school setting, it is common for a dean (like me) to instruct a staff member who reports directly to me to keep objections to a change to herself or himself once a decision has been made and to model the change outwardly. And yet I would hesitate to say the same to a faculty member, who is in many ways a peer, and who is protected by societal expectations that professors are entitled to freedom to express their ideas. With them, instructions to support the school publicly tend to backfire. Kotter's advice that the "guiding coalition model the behavior expected of employees" is important in faith communities just as it is in other institutions, but when the bottom line is human and communal transformation, authenticity is sometimes more important than a unified front.

5. Empowering broad-based action. Kotter writes that "getting rid of obstacles" and "[c]hanging systems or structures that undermine the change vision" are important in change leadership. He also advocates for taking risks and thinking outside the proverbial box. This advice is perhaps most important for organizations that promote love for tradition the way faith communities do and must. At one extreme, communities hoard permission to bring about change in the community, fearing identity loss and lacking trust in innovation's effects on tradition. At the other extreme, organizations cavalierly dismiss traditional practices, not knowing why they were instituted or how they might still be important. In my experience, a community will be open to change if they trust that the leader is not going throw out babies with bathwater. Sometimes leaders feel offended or hurt when they are not trusted automatically or immediately. It helps when they accept that trust-building not only takes time, but lack of trust resurfaces in waves when change is afoot. Even long-time leaders must cultivate and earn trust regularly, even daily.

6. Generating short-term wins. Religious leaders do not think in terms of winning and losing, and perhaps that is one of many reasons why they do not typically build visible signals of success into change initiatives. They need to, because those signals matter greatly to change efforts. As of the time of this writing, I am preparing for a meeting where board members want to hear about how our school's new venture—over which the board toiled and on which the board took a significant risk—is unfolding. I have to set aside any natural tendencies and hard-won lessons that steer me away from inviting the board to count chickens before they have hatched. The board needs reassurance that they did the right thing, as well as encouragement to invest more energy into the new venture.

I caution leaders of faith communities against trotting out numbers of participants as their sole short-term win. "We have ten new members since we added the nursery" is a short-term win asking for trouble. Numbers do matter, but their usefulness as signs of success is limited. Why? Because we must constantly remind our communities that our bottom line is human and communal transformation toward God's vision for us. Numbers of participants can too easily become the vision, rather than a part of the vision, because human beings crave simplistic evidence of success.

As my husband Dan is wont to say, in relation to his role as a college guidance counselor, "Don't take credit now unless you're ready to take blame later." Numbers are not where you want blame to happen. Visual and emotional signals of success are often more effective. For instance, instead of counting membership noses after a nursery is added, ask parents to populate a bulletin board with baby pictures as a thank you to the congregation who made the nursery possible. Short-term wins in faith communities cannot be tallied entirely quantitatively, but they must be lifted up and celebrated with intentionality: it is the wins that energize the leaders who need to be ready for more change.

7. **Consolidating gains and producing more change.** How tempting it is for faith community leaders to say, "We brought about a change, and now we are finished with that!" And yet the fast pace of change in our culture suggests that as soon as one initiative unfolds, another needs to follow immediately. A changing culture is a new normal for leaders. Consider this fable:[22] a peasant went to the emperor to discuss his wages for work on the emperor's land. The peasant arranged that, instead of a sack of rice per month, he would be paid using the squares on the landowner's chess board for a formula: in the first square in the first row, the emperor would place one grain of rice, and that would be the peasant's first week's wages. The second square, the portion would be doubled; in the third square, the amount from the second square doubled, and so on. The emperor thought this arrangement was

---

22 The fable could be of Chinese or Indian origin and dates back nearly to the invention of chess itself. Retrieved 6.26.2018 from https://www.clustre.net/digital-abundance-and-the-second-half-of-the-chessboard/.

to his advantage, so he agreed to the peasant's terms. Soon, however, the peasant had claim to all the rice in the landowner's granary due to the exponential growth of the rice portions over time.

Futurists say that we, as a global culture in the twenty-first century, are living in the second half of the chessboard. Change happened rapidly in the twentieth century, but today change takes place at breakneck speed. We have to organize our communities in a manner that predicts change's pace will continue to accelerate. Once we introduce a change, we have to get through it, and past it, and onto the next change. Slow change was once understood as the only effective kind, but the slowness was not what mattered; what mattered was the consolidating work involved in anchoring the change in the culture, which can be either fast or slow. We now know that slow change has downsides that are getting more and more dangerous for institutions. Slow change used to be considered careful and faithful. Now it is much like putting one's money in a mattress rather than investing it in the stock market: stocks might rise and fall, but a mattress stuffed with money will do nothing but prevent a good night's sleep.

8. Anchoring new approaches in the culture. Where companies might anchor change in the organization's culture through changing corporate customs, language, and structures, religious leaders anchor change in theology. I am part of a board that is embarking on a significant revision of its bylaws. In discussions about that new project, I raised the following point vis-à-vis language related to change: "We know that we need to do 'things' 'differently.' We become intolerably anxious when we focus on the 'differently.' We become encouraged when we focus on the 'things.'" What does this play on words mean? It means that faith communities must dedicate attention to that which is *essential* to their purpose and identity before deciding how to live out that purpose and identity. Theology is at the heart of "things" done by faith communities.

The institution I serve has a 211-year history of educating clergy. "Educating" has taken on many different shapes over the 2,000-year history of the church, with seminaries only existing for the later portion of that time period. "Clergy" is a designation for authorized servants of God that has taken many forms, starting with the early church. In my own context, I have attempted to avoid assuming I and other leaders are all on the same wavelength about "educating" and "clergy," rushing hastily into "doing things differently." I suggest that we should dwell more fully in the meaning of those two core words to my setting's identity. Focus there: what is most important? What is essential? What is good? Only then can we decide what to do the same, differently, or not at all.

Anchoring change in the culture requires tethering the change onto that which is eternal, or at least essential. In faith communities, which love tradition, the leader must demonstrate in word and deed that change is necessary if we are to honor values we wish would stay the same. In other words, the new practice introduced must be deemed *more appropriate* to the essential character of the institution than what was being done before. The change that is different for differentness's sake is doomed. The change that is connected to the central purpose of the faith community, and is arguably more appropriate to meeting the community's goals, can be as drastic as drastic can be. Making the connection between the change and the organization's purpose anchors that change in the culture.

It is here, in Kotter's last stage, where we can see the cycle resume, as anchoring leads directly back to visioning. A strong sense of vision, in which the community is invested, is the strongest motivator in furthering and anchoring change in the culture of an institution. If the community for the most part believes in the vision (100 percent satisfaction is never guaranteed, but 85 percent or 90 percent is essential), those within it will tolerate it. If they have not bought in, they will be willing to change very little, or nothing at all. They will find reasons to stall, to resist, and to sabotage, as the emotions that resist change will overpower a weak rational motivation. It is here we see the intersection of reason and emotion, for emotion and reason coexist in ways that cannot be cleanly separated.

Adaptive versus Technical Change Leadership

As described earlier, Harvard Business School's Ronald Heifetz defines leadership to his students as the practice of moving a community from a less than adequate status quo, through disequilibrium, to a new and more satisfactory status quo. A better-known and deceptively simple theory Heifetz presents is the difference between technical and adaptive change.[23] An organization can make a technical change in its surroundings, but an adaptive change requires leaders to change themselves. Consider the following fictional, but surely all too common illustration:

A college with older buildings is not wheelchair accessible. It has no elevator or ramps, door frames require pulling to open, and toilets in the bathroom are close together and separated by narrow stalls. Technically, the community needs money to pay for design, labor, and supplies. Adaptively, the college's leaders must think in a new way. Why? Because the first objection that will come up when proposing the technical changes will sound something like, "But we don't have any students in wheelchairs at the school." The first response will be, "Well, of course we don't! We're not accessible." And then the misery will ensue, as those who have remained focused on technical fixes are not able to reason together. This misery is inevitable in the absence of a leader capable of guiding a community toward looking deeply at itself, its values, and its possibilities. We need to think differently.

---

23 Heifetz, *Leadership without Easy Answers.*

Heifetz writes that many a leadership failure has resulted from treating an adaptive issue, which must take place through the leader seeing things differently, with a technical one. Technical fixes do not foster adaptive change. Carrying the preceding illustration a step further, consider the results of the Americans with Disabilities Act, which requires that any significant renovation to a building owned by an institution that receives federal funds to include plans for becoming accessible. This is, technically, a good thing: organizations that have the resources for a renovation must conform to the law whether they have prioritized inclusion or not. By turning accessibility from a justice matter into a legal matter, however, organizations do not have to do the hard work of searching their souls. They might therefore take the technical step without adaptive adjustment, meaning that the next time an access issue comes up, they will be back at the proverbial square one. Does this make the ADA law around renovations a bad law? Of course not. But the deeper work of adaptation is necessary for meaningful, long-lasting change. When foregone, adaptive work remains for another day.

Throughout his years of writing and teaching, Heifetz advocated leading change at a rate that a community can tolerate without burnout or rupture. Earlier in his career, that truism gave one the impression that Heifetz advocated for the maximum amount of change an organization can tolerate. When an oncologist prescribes aggressive chemotherapy, they will give the patient the highest dosage possible, with the upper threshold being the level of side-effects the patient can survive. Finding that intersection point between the most medication the patient can tolerate and the worst side-effects the patient can endure is the doctor's art and science to master. For decades, Heifetz's teachings suggested that leaders' art and science were similar.

In 2011, I had the opportunity to hear Heifetz sing a different song when he offered a leadership workshop for clergy hosted by my seminary. He shared some of his more recent work that, like previous writings, used organismal biology. This time, the metaphor was DNA. Now that scientists can map DNA sequences in organisms, we know that even the most minor changes to a strand produce massive changes. Splice out a tiny portion of the sequence, and you change the organism from one species to another. Splice out the tiniest bit more, and the organism can no longer support life. Diseases like cancer result from the slightest of mutations. Might simply tweaking programs and organizations have more than a tweaking effect?

Tweaking is, in my experience of leadership, underrated. Organizations that try to resolve giant problems with small tweaks are doomed, we hear, and their leaders must lack courage. Heifetz's more recent work with the metaphor of DNA suggests otherwise. A small change, a tweak here or there, can have a catalytic effect that permeates the whole organization. The question is not whether tweaking is enough, but what kind of tweaks result in a chain reaction toward more life? Heifetz is not the only author who concerns himself with leadership practices that give communities change at a rate they can stand, but the arc of his writings suggests that he has rethought how sweeping change must be in order to make a meaningful difference.

To make small, strategic changes is a brave and effective leadership undertaking, not one that lacks bold vision, as some might wrongly assume. In an article entitled "A Grain of Wheat: Toward a Theological Anthropology for Leading Change in Ministry," Bard Eirik Hallesby Norheim writes that humans are made up in equal measure of "historicity" and "plasticity."[24] Historicity signifies the ways in which human beings transcend time, embodying a past and present and future that connect them to something greater than

---

24 Bård Eirik Hallesby Norheim, "A Grain of Wheat: Toward a Theological Anthropology for Leading Change in Ministry," *Journal of Religious Leadership* 13, no. 1 (2014): 68–77.

themselves. Plasticity represents the ways in which human beings can and do change over the course of their lifetimes. Norheim cites theologian Kathryn Tanner's work when claiming that the event of the cross is the primary inspiration a Christian can invoke as evidence that anything God creates can be transformed. Leaders do well to consider balancing a community's historicity with its plasticity: you have a history, and you can change. Norheim writes that change theory that emerges from the business world considers a vision the way a Greek philosopher would consider *telos*: it is an ideal end-point. Theologians are different from philosophers. They claim that the inspiration for transformation is not teleological but eschatological (see chapter 5): the end of days will not become a more ideal version of reality as we know it, but rather it will be God's time. A theological perspective places Christ at the center of change rather than leaders themselves.

By this reasoning, we can see that the most important differences between a secular and a sacred change effort are the means and the ends. The means: uncover Christ's will, relying on the Holy Spirit, for Christ's will points us to God's imagination for us. The ends: life triumphing over death. Whether the change is big or small, the changes we make reflect what we understand to be God's vision for our communities, rendering none of our actions—no matter how small—insignificant.

Change leadership is not the first place I have encountered a Greek ideal confusing to Christians. My first significant research was in religion and higher education, where Christian chaplains seek to find their role in organizations that might have been founded to educate clergy. Because the Greek ideal elevates contemplation over activity,[25] higher educational institutions tacitly reward those who get their hands least dirty. They relegate

---

[25] Palmer, *The Active Life: A Spirituality of Work, Creativity, and Caring* (San Francisco: Jossey-Bass, 1999).

those who are most carnally, messily, and actively engaged with the work of the university to the bottom of the hierarchy.

Similarly, change leaders who are formed in this Greek ideal engage in what I called in *Holy Clarity* the pietistic fantasy: that someone else will take care of the messes, while I lead from my lofty place.[26] All this to say that when telos and eschaton coexist, the tie goes to the telos. Religious leaders have to be exceedingly intentional in their efforts to reframe issues in Christian terms, where life's triumph is the end goal, not the all-important Greek ideal of being above the mess, and right.

Like Norheim, Lorraine Ste-Marie writes about the ways in which a change theory rooted in reason can be reinterpreted to serve a Christian framework. In an article "'Immunity-to-Change Language Technology': An Educational Tool for Pastoral Leadership Education,"[27] Ste-Marie describes a pastoral leadership education method built on Kegan's *Immunity to Change*. She makes the case that pastoral leadership involves the student taking the risk of delving into that which is keeping them from effective ministry. They do so through exploring their own resistances and finding the nonchange motivation pulling against their best efforts to change. The biblical inspiration Ste-Marie finds for this difficult work is Luke 5:1–11, here quoted from the New Revised Standard Version:

> Once while Jesus was standing beside the lake of Gennesaret, and the crowd was pressing in on him to hear the word of God, he saw two boats there at the shore of the lake; the fishermen had gone out of them and were washing their nets. He got into one of the boats, the one belonging to Simon, and asked him to put out a little way from the shore. Then he sat down and taught the

---

26 Drummond, *Holy Clarity*, 22.

27 Lorraine Ste-Marie, "'Immunity-to-Change Language Technology': An Educational Tool for Pastoral Leadership Education," *Teaching Theology and Religion* 11, no. 2 (2008):92–108.

crowds from the boat. When he had finished speaking, he said to Simon, "Put out into the deep water and let down your nets for a catch." Simon answered, "Master, we have worked all night long but have caught nothing. Yet if you say so, I will let down the nets." When they had done this, they caught so many fish that their nets were beginning to break. So they signaled to their partners in the other boat to come and help them. And they came and filled both boats, so that they began to sink. But when Simon Peter saw it, he fell down at Jesus's knees, saying, "Go away from me, Lord, for I am a sinful man!" For he and all who were with him were amazed at the catch of fish that they had taken; and so also were James and John, sons of Zebedee, who were partners with Simon. Then Jesus said to Simon, "Do not be afraid; from now on you will be catching people." When they had brought their boats to shore, they left everything and followed him.

Put out into the deep, writes Ste-Marie, to find what it is you are looking for. Jesus told you that in doing so, you have nothing to fear.

Norheim's biblical framework comes from an altogether different idea found in John 12:24 that reads, "Very truly, I tell you, unless a grain of wheat falls into the earth and dies, it remains just a single grain; but if it dies, it bears much fruit." Norheim makes the case that what frightens Christians most about the prospect of change is the fear of death. Although he does not explicitly cite Paul Tillich, his ideas about the fear of oblivion mirror that of Tillich and other twentieth-century theologians whose experience of the Second World War raised existential questions about ultimacy and our fear of it. Selecting the parable of the grain of wheat, rather than Jesus's death on the cross, seems significant. A nature image selected by Jesus to articulate how death and life are intertwined provides a framework for accepting death as part of life—ending as part of changing—that is less terrifying and thus more amenable to theological reflection than Christ's own resurrection. Reasoning results in hard, cold truths. Faith overcomes our fear of facing those truths.

Christ's own resurrection was and is the ultimate example and guide for life triumphing over death. In the seminary in which I lead, one of the hardest decisions we have ever made was the one to give up a campus that we loved on a beautiful hill. The campus was too big for us, falling down around our ears with deferred maintenance and bleeding us dry financially, yet giving it up was among the most painful processes the school has ever experienced. It was not the first campus our school has given up, and I often wondered if those who made a similar decision in the nineteenth century experienced some of the same fears of oblivion.

On many occasions, those of us in leadership at the school needed to frame the work of closing one campus and opening another one in theological language. Just as often, we had to respond to the frameworks presented by others. In one forum for alumni, one of our alums used the theological metaphor of "emptying," in which we as a school were letting go of our campus in order that God might fill us with what we needed. This was a theological framing that worked for me. In several other settings, and even from the mouths of our faculty, we heard Good Friday imagery, which I personally found painful. I was of course dealing with my own grief, which was a difficult thing to address while hard at work on ensuring that students could graduate, and that our school would have a next chapter. As I was taking comfort in the idea that people of faith had relocated in order to flourish over the centuries, death and resurrection were simply too emotionally drastic for me. I needed to continue to function, so narratives that included death and rebirth as an ordinary part of life were a comfort to me.

Norheim might say that we as administrative leaders were predictably resistant to the idea that change requires death, and perhaps he would be right, but I resonated right away with Norheim's metaphor of a grain of wheat that must fall and take root before new life can flourish. Ste-Marie's framework for significant change, where she borrows Kegan's language of immunity-to-change and creates a pastoral development exercise of it, is even more satisfying. In the case of my institution, we wanted to be free to educate religious leaders in new, creative, and relevant ways. What was keeping us from doing so was constant worry about a bottom-line whose balance simply could not improve under the weight of the burdens we were carrying.

This chapter dedicated to the rational and sense-making dimensions of change leadership therefore finds theological footing on two metaphorical foundations: resurrection and conversion. Jesus's resurrection carries many meanings for Christians. In the case of individual and communal change, we are reminded that life triumphs over death by virtue of Jesus's resurrection. His resurrection is not just a metaphor or an example related to what happens after death. It is that which carves out the path for us to come back to life throughout our lives: mini-resurrections that take place after mini-deaths. A loss of a loved one through death, a relationship rupture, a failure, or a catastrophe: any of these can cause us to think that life is over. And then we find out—God teaches us—that it is not.

A second theological foundation is that of conversion. We face the wrong direction, watching the wrong signs, listening to the wrong voices. Through Jesus's teachings, and the occasional tough-love intervention from the Holy Spirit, we turn around and face that which God intends for us. That turning around can be painful and slow, or painful and fast. Conversion turns us away from death-dealing ways and toward a direction that brings new life.

An interior change of heart, conversion has distinctive marks in a person or organization's behavior. Once we let go of some habits that were taking us in the wrong direction, we become braver and shed old skin.

We encounter resistance from those who do not see the death-dealing way, or from those who have a different idea about that toward which we should turn. Therefore, communication about what a person or leader is trying to accomplish by moving in a new direction is essential, for no two people convert in the same way. Hearkening back to theories of change, everyone has a different idea of what is the appropriate change to make. Describing the motivations behind our choices to turn in a new direction is essential, for conversion's logic is by nature an internal one.

The leader relies on leadership steps that are essential for breaking apart the soil upon which seeds will fall, and then steps for cultivating—developing—those seeds toward the best possibility that they will take root and grow. In this next section of the chapter, I will describe specific actions leaders take when approaching change leadership from a cognitive-developmental direction. In the church community or religious institution, the minister leads change in part by teaching. She makes sense of the realities surrounding her in the community and beyond, shares that sense-making with the community in conversation, leadership meetings, preaching, writing, and any other outlet she can find. She learns the context, the stories, and the life events that have shaped the community into being what it is. During that time of intentional learning, she is most active in her work as lover of souls: encouraging, supporting, drying tears, sharing successes, and becoming connected. In carrying out these duties, she learns the community's story and then relays it back to the people.

Teaching takes varied shapes in different settings. Effective teaching relies on connectedness that comes from the religious leader's work as one who loves. Parker Palmer writes that the definition of effective teaching is, "only connect."[28] A teacher can lecture without taking a breath or accepting questions, or he can open up the floor for vibrant discussion. He can use a manuscript or fly by the seat of his pants. But he must connect, and only connect, if his message is to have any impact at all. The leader teaches through connecting, building a bridge between themselves and the community, and between members of the community and one another. Through that connection, they describe reality as it is through any means available.

How does the leader even know enough about the nature of a community's reality to have the confidence to share that status boldly and broadly? Lo, if every leader were to be so humble as to ask that question! Leaders sometimes jump to conclusions. They bring their own agendas and are easily frustrated when their ideas are not embraced. They are quick to call others jerks, as ministerial leadership scholar Arthur Boers has written.[29] Boers argues, of course, never do that. Rather, ask the question: what am I missing? How can I connect?

Assessment and Leadership

In order that leaders can be sufficiently informed about the needs of their communities, they must conduct an assessment. Although assessments take different forms—private and public, informal and formal—they are a necessary step. In a complex cultural moment, only the most arrogant leader trusts their gut in reading a community. We assess using disciplines of learning, not a combination of eyeballing communities and projecting our assumptions onto them.

Disciplines of assessment begin with this series of questions: "What is it that we, as a community or organization, say we do?

---

28 Parker J. Palmer, *The Courage to Teach* (San Francisco: Jossey-Bass, 1998).

29 Arthur Boers, *Never Call Them Jerks* (Bethesda, MD: Alban Institute, 1999).

What do we actually do? When there are disconnects, what will we change: what we say, or what we do?" We find answers to these questions using the following three practices for collecting data: interviews, focus groups, and document review. Interviews can take the form of formal, scheduled conversations with the purpose of deeply understanding the life of an organization. Some leaders make a point, in their first year, of sitting down individually with each constituent. Others use ordinary conversations for the purpose of ongoing learning.

Focus groups are similar to interviews, but the purpose is to get constituents talking to each other so the leader can listen in. One way leaders can convene focus groups is by piggybacking on already scheduled meetings for teams and committees, asking for a few minutes of reflective sharing. Document review can be as simple as reading the files available in the office to get a sense of an organization's history. It can be as complicated as commissioning a history of a church or a demographic study of a faith community's surrounding area.

Typically, practices of assessment are easier for leaders who are newer to their roles. When a relatively new leader asks, "Why do we do it that way?" the question does not sound confrontational, and no one wonders if "it" might be on the chopping block. A newer leader who states she wants to sit down with every member of the community individually for a conversation is seen as conscientious and caring, where a continuing leader might seem to have a secret agenda. Although the practices associated with assessment might seem less awkward for leaders new to their settings, I have tended to find that I need time to become familiar with a community before assessment practices help me. For example, reading a policy document—say, a set of bylaws—when we are new to a setting might wash over us. Reading it after many meeting experiences is more informative: where are the bylaws in effect, where are they ignored, how could they improve? I have often returned to policy documents I thought I knew two and three years into a new position and found them incredibly useful, as if for the first time.

Assessment leads to a new narrative about that which we boldly call "reality." The leader describes reality and compares their sense of it with espoused narratives held by others in the community. Once we have a relatively clear picture of what is happening in a faith community, we are ready to consider the next question: how does our current reality match, or fail to match, what we understand to be God's vision for the community? In other words, what do we have to do to create a new reality that conforms more closely with God's imagination?

As was described earlier in the chapter, few leadership practices must involve the whole community but for visioning. Once that vision is arrived upon, leaders carry the ball without complete participation from every constituent, but if we believe that God's imagination is made known to us all, we must give all an opportunity to bring their voices to the new narrative.

Convinced that visioning best happens with the whole of the community, what is next? Ministry requires management of large-group dynamics. How can we promote a sense of belonging and inclusion for a large group of people who are different from each other? Plenary discussions, where individuals take turns talking and listening, are but one—and a flawed one—way of gathering a group together to construct a new communal vision. Here are two more: Appreciative Inquiry and a World Café. Appreciative Inquiry,[30] a leadership practice pioneered and championed by scholars from Case Western Reserve University, calls upon leaders to promote the best energies of a community. Through inquiring as to the most positive feelings, experiences, and accomplishments

---

[30] Read more about Appreciative Inquiry at https://www.centerforappreciativeinquiry.net/ (accessed June 27, 2018).

of a community, constituents find themselves stimulated to make more good happen. A simple "AI" exercise might look like this: gather the community together. Pair participants in groups of two. The two ask each other, "What is a story you can remember of this community fully alive?" The pair takes turns speaking and listening. The group then comes back together, and the facilitator asks participants to share not what they or their partner said, but what they learned about what God is calling the community to become.

World Café is similar. Originating in leadership circles in California, World Café[31] styles of large-group facilitation break down barriers between people as well as different forms of knowing. Consider this example of a World Café visioning session: a space usually used for meetings is reorganized into small tables with four chairs around each. On the tables are large pieces of paper and multicolored markers. Each table includes a broad, guiding question, written in the center of the paper. Questions might be, "What is your favorite thing about this community?" "Whom are we here to serve?" "What about this community do you believe is pleasing to God?" Participants are encouraged to enjoy snacks and beverages and bring them to their tables. The facilitator explains that they are to stay at different tables for fifteen-minute increments and discuss the guiding question with whomever is there, eating their snacks and doodling their impressions of the discussion if they wish. At the transitions, the facilitator encourages people to try to sit with different configurations of people. After three rounds, the facilitator asks that the sheets of paper be displayed around the café-like space, and participants walk around to look at the papers as though at an art exhibit. Then in plenary, the group shares what they have learned about the community's developing mental picture of a new reality.

---

[31] Read more about World Café at http://www.theworldcafe.com/key-concepts-resources/world-cafe-method/ (accessed June 27, 2018).

These two practices, like the Polaroid exercise described previously, help us to draw out the community's imagination. It is all too easy, however, to define "community" narrowly without thinking through who its true stakeholders might be. It is for this reason that I have written elsewhere about the importance of disciplined stakeholder mapping.[32] A simple exercise to help leaders to broaden their understanding of stakeholders is to ask them to list every individual and every group who would rightly have a reason to care about the work of a community. Then they map out who is directly, indirectly, and only incidentally affected using a map that looks like a dart board (see Figure 2.1).

By linking the list with the map, communities can ask questions like "How might those in the outer circles contribute to visioning? How might their imaginations expose leaders to dimensions of the community's work they might otherwise have missed?"

Through teaching the leader deepens the community's knowledge of the vision's importance and its theological grounding. They find every available means to instruct the community on the way in which the new vision makes sense. But the leader cannot stop there, expecting that imparting wisdom is enough to carry the community from a current—perhaps insufficient—reality to a new one more pleasing to God. The leader might embrace a fantasy that, as long as the vision is a good one, and the people carrying it out reasonable people, they need do no more. Sadly, they are wrong.

The second essential leadership discipline that corresponds to a reasoned approach to change leadership is planning. The vision is at the heart of a planning process, but that heart needs a body and a mind. Here is a simple planning exercise (Table 2.1) that demonstrates how a plan flows from the vision. It is a version of a logic model[33] that is a commonly used tool in program planning and evaluation.

---

32 Drummond, *Holy Clarity*, 63.

33 Ibid., 60–61.

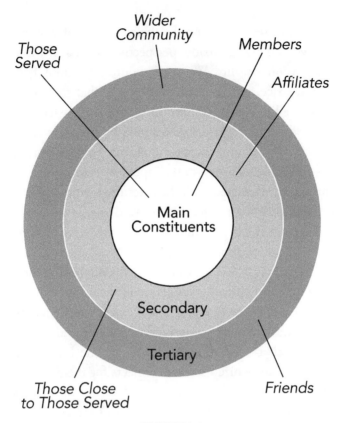

FIGURE 2.1

Resources	Inputs	Outputs	Realized Vision	Outward Signs
What do we bring to the change?	What do we do?	What happens?	What results?	How will be know those results have taken place?

TABLE 2.1

As you can see in column 4, labeled "Realized Vision: What results?" we find here a broader perspective on what it will take to make the vision a reality. We need resources (column 1) such as the money, space, staff, or volunteer energy that the community possesses. We list inputs (column 2) that describe what leaders of various kinds actually do, using column 1's resources along with their efforts. We examine outputs (column 3), which are the net effects—the consequences—of the inputs. We consider the inward transformation associated with those results—actualization of the vision (column 4)—through the outward signs (column 5) that indicate the vision is becoming reality. It is the outward signs upon which an evaluation process can focus.

The leader must teach the community, reminding them constantly in new and different ways, to look at the big picture and to think the vision all the way through. Where there are logical flaws on the pathway between the resources available and the outward signs for which the community is hoping, the leader helps the community to recognize those disconnects for themselves. When the community has a vision that excites them but the prospects for carrying that vision out are grim, the leader's job can be unpleasant. The leader can keep lifting up reality and offering alternative paths.

If visioning is so powerful and ambitious planning so realistic when a vision is embraced, why do so few communities undertake it? Perhaps one answer lies in the work of twentieth-century sociologist Abraham Maslow, who argued that we can only begin to consider self-actualization when our more basic needs for safety and bodily sustenance are met. Maslow suggested a hierarchy of needs, where bodily survival must be certain before higher attainments in meaning-making are possibilities.[34] By that logic, only

---

[34] I have picked up Maslow's theory over the years through exposure to it, not through studying it, but I have found the idea that institutions cannot act creatively when under existential threat to be persuasive and helpful.

the community that feels safe can dream. In a time when institutions are subject to newly intense levels of scrutiny, sometimes fairly and sometimes unfairly, stress levels run high. Leaders can go a long way, through their teaching and their planning, to help the community to feel safe enough to vision.

As soon as we have a logic model for change, we can make a timeline and assign responsibilities. What needs to be done, in what sequence, and by what time, in order for the hoped-for outputs to occur? What resources are available, and what resources must be identified and secured? Charting out the steps in the timeline is one way of ensuring we do not lose momentum as a vision comes into focus. Losing momentum is a terrible waste, for it is at the moment when a vision is fresh and exciting that energy is highest and fear lowest. The community is only all too briefly more excited about what might be gained than they are afraid of the possible grief in store for them. Breaking a complex vision down into manageable steps—for example, by drafting a specific, color-coded timeline— helps the guiding coalition to stay calm and helps the community overcome its fear of the future. By color-coding steps in the timeline according to who will carry each step out, all know their responsibilities, and accountability is built in from the start.

The Evaluation-Ready Change Initiative

Also from the start, leaders need to create a plan for evaluation. "Wait," you might be thinking. "Why would you need to build an evaluation plan for something that has not even happened yet?" Because, as an old saying goes, "If you don't know what you're aiming for, you'll hit it every time." Evaluation practices designed from the inception point of change force the message that focus, goal-setting, and specificity are important. A simple evaluation plan can build on the logic model's Indicators column in Table 2.2.[35]

---

[35] Drummond, *Holy Clarity*, 66.

Outward Signs (column 5 in Table 2.1)	Data Sources	Collection Plan	Analysis Strategy
Indicators that a change has taken place	Artifacts in the form of documents, spoken words, numbers	Strategy for collecting artifacts at appropriate intervals	Plan for interpreting and disseminating findings

TABLE 2.2

By "artifacts," I do not mean fossils. I mean pieces of evidence that are like pieces in a puzzle. When put together, they tell a story, even though the shape of each is different.

Imagine a change initiative that involves creating a youth center in a vacant space in a church building. One indicator of success might be the number of youth who come through on a daily basis to do homework and play games. Another indicator might be the satisfaction and happiness of kids while at the youth center. These indicators are equally measurable. The evaluator who says that happiness is not quantifiable is being needlessly officious: anything that can be described can be measured with some effort and creativity. A data source for happiness in the youth center might be the youth themselves, and their adult leaders.

Were I to measure happiness in such a circumstance, I would make sheets of stickers with facial expressions on them and ask participants, when they sign out, to use a sticker to indicate how they are feeling. The number of smiley faces equals how happy they are: measurement problem solved. Of course, interviewing kids, observing them, creating focus groups, and distributing surveys work too. Rich understandings can emerge from a wide array of data gathering practices.

Collecting data is just the beginning. Leaders need to think about what it is they want to learn about the impact of the program, what they will do with the artifacts they gather by way of analysis, and what they might be willing to adjust based on what they learn. Therefore, having an analysis strategy from the start is similarly clarifying. The program plan is all the better for leaders having taken the time to really think through what they are seeking to accomplish when planning a change.

An evaluative practice common for seminary student interns in theological field education is the discipline of theological reflection. In the field education program I co-led at Andover Newton, students in supervised ministry chose a critical incident every week. They created two-column documents, where a description of the event appeared on the left and their theological reflections appeared on the right. Those reflections have included scripture, theological concepts, pastoral care issues, and other connections between the event and what the students were learning in seminary. By holding up incidents in the light of faith, students formed analytical habits for self-evaluation and seeing the world through the lenses of their faith traditions. Evaluative practices like theological reflection can apply to a program just as easily as they do an individual minister's experience. What happened, and where do we see God in what happened? These habits of mind form leaders to use reason to lead change without losing track of what faith communities seek to achieve.

Perhaps even reading all these different steps in planning a change initiative feels overwhelming, slow, ponderous, untrusting of God, and not fun. "Why can't we just do it and see what happens?" Of course, you can, and sometimes making a foray is a great idea. None of the steps named in this section—visioning, making a timeline, creating an evaluation plan—need to happen in the sequence described, nor must they take inordinate amounts of time. Sometimes just giving something new a shot and letting the chips fall where they may is a way to capitalize on energy for the change that might not last long enough for the hard work just described. Sometimes the first step needs to be action, and we backfill the steps named in this chapter in order to anchor change. That said, momentum is to be respected but not revered. If a change was thinly owned by a community that was not patient enough to deepen its thinking about change, it is possible that inertia will reassert itself all the more stubbornly when energies move elsewhere.

Reason is essential not only to create a new change initiative, but also to review a change that has already been made, especially when the change is not becoming reality the way that leaders had hoped. A logic model can help leaders to see where a change effort when wrong. They might ascertain, for example, that they attempted a change without sufficient resources. Or that they had assumed certain outputs without determining who would provide the inputs. Using a logic model to make sense of a ministry situation gone wrong is no parlor game. What happens when the reality the analysis lays bare is awful? What if it indicates the change would never work, or that a particular party screwed up royally?

Fear—especially fear of failure—presents a formidable obstacle to reasoned analysis of an organization and its need for change. Fear's attendants, grief and anxiety, provide ample reasons why a leader might never want to change anything. The whole field of leadership consulting is built around the idea that it is sometimes necessary to have an external presence truthfully examine an institution's reality, as those who are deeply invested will not be able to look too hard at it for its sheer painfulness. In the next chapter, I explore how emotion contributes to this particular form of being overwhelmed, but here I will focus on the necessity of supports, health, and spiritual practices to the capacity to use reason to bring about change.

Reason relies on empirical truths: that which can be measured and quantified and subjected to logic. Many religious leaders shy away from reason-based leadership because of its coldness, preferring to focus more on feelings and relationships. Doing so is like a baker shying away from using a pan to make a cake. By avoiding truth and reason, we lose the space where collaboration takes place, and we end up with a big mess. As Rabbi Edwin Friedman wrote, the leader who is accused of being cold is probably doing something right.[36] The leader who is accused of saying aloud a community's hard realities is doing the job, and it is not an easy one.

Leaders who are going to be truthful also have to be attentive to matters of mental, spiritual, and physical health. They must have colleagues and friends with whom they consult regularly for reality checks, honest talk, laughter, and kindness. Fitness and other practices of wellness are necessary so a leader stays grounded through the body. Mental health care through therapy that specifically addresses emotions, understanding where they come from, and listening to them rather than reacting to them? Essential.

For many years, I have assigned seminary students projects where they profile a minister who is thriving. One of the questions I encourage the groups to ask their profilees is, "How do you take care of yourself?" The responses astound the students. They expect to hear that self-care is low on the list, and that is how the minister has been so successful. They expect to hear from those who are truly attentive to caring for their well-being that about twenty minutes a day is enough. On the contrary: the thriving ministers spend two and three hours a day working out, having fun with their families, and engaging hobbies. Even when controlling for how wealthy or financially strapped the ministries served are, the pattern has been unmistakable: thriving leaders profiled take excellent care of themselves. If they do not, the consequence is that they cannot see the truth.

---

36 Edwin Friedman, *A Failure of Nerve: Leadership in the Age of the Quick Fix* (New York: Church Publishing, 1999, 2007).

Because the truth can be distressing. Often, leaders who are planted on solid ground can take in realities around them that those they lead do not see, and about which they do not want to hear. In order to avoid hurtful realities, constituents kill the messengers or ignore the messages. I recently saw a news story about a building in San Francisco that is sinking. A luxurious and ridiculously heavy high-rise condominium tower was not built on a foundation anchored on bedrock. As the building tips to the side and heads deeper into the ground, those who bought condos in it cannot find buyers and cannot get comfortable in their living spaces, where pencils roll off desks and doors hang from their hinges at odd angles.

The metaphor of a beautiful building whose foundation was insufficiently deep reminded me of many leaders I know, and also reminded me of myself at various points in my life and ministry. From a distance, the building looks to be of high quality, and in terms of its materials, it is. On closer inspection, there are disconnects and fissures that indicate a lack of grounding. Just like a sinking building, it is the long-term one worries about: the structure will not fall over tomorrow, but it is not built for the long haul.

The bedrock on which a religious leader's structure is built is the life of faith. Like the faith life of all people, religious leaders' faith changes over the course of lifetimes. Our theologies evolve and our practices vary based on circumstances and opportunities in our context. It would be impossible to overstate the importance to the leader of spiritual practices that keep the leader connected to the divine. I hesitate to make the argument that faith leaders must be deeply grounded in their spiritual practice in order to be effective in their work, lest I instrumentalize faith toward some worldly purpose. Similarly, I do not like to admit that part of the reason I exercise is because I want to be slender. Suffice it to say that both spirituality and physical fitness are good for us in many ways.

In the case of spiritual groundedness: its goodness inheres and is sufficient unto itself. That faith in God helps us to stay strong when the world around us is in turmoil, and helps us to tell even the most unpopular of truths, is grace upon grace. Jesus turned to God when his followers frustrated him and could not see the truth. Jesus taught us to do the same, so we do.

 ## Exercise: Visioning in Groups

Throughout this chapter, I have argued that it is important for the entire community to have a role in a visioning process. The widest possible conversation about visioning has many benefits: the vision will be more accurate and also more creative; it will have more investment from the wider community; and it will be a more adequate reflection of God's vision for having included God's children. Why is it so difficult, then, to have such a broad conversation? Because our institutional systems are not always built first and foremost for inclusivity. The following practices help leaders to carry out a wide-ranging visioning process. Reach back into the chapter to remind yourself of the following group processes for visioning and planning, each of which relies on communicating and teaching:

- Stakeholder Mapping
- Appreciative Inquiry
- World Café
- Logic Modeling
- Evaluation Plans
- Timelines

 ## Exercise: Reasoning Together

If all you have by way of understanding the nature of an institution is a business, you look at your church as though it were a business, and it is not. At times, religious leaders underestimate the spiritual depth and need for vision among business leaders. Business leaders sometimes underestimate their ministers' savvy. How can we help them to understand each other better?

Reason-oriented change leadership resembles change perspectives from the business world. How can we celebrate similarities and differences between ministries and businesses? By reasoning together. Leaders among institutions have similar goals and concerns, and when they work together, great things can happen. This exercise can help leaders to explore the practical similarities and differences between leadership in settings motivated by different goals, in this case, corporate profit versus human and communal transformation (Table 2.3). It is useful for groups that will be working together and need to understand how they are different from one another so they can focus in on shared goals.

Institutional Goals	Unique to Market	Unique to Ministry	Similar for Both
• Success			
• Efficiency			
• Innovation			
• Transparency			
• Social Justice			
• Interpersonal fairness			
• Quality			
• Relevance			

TABLE 2.3

Gifts for Change Leadership

An effective leader amidst change is organized and communicative.
A reason-based perspective on change tells us that planning and
teaching are what help navigate a community toward a life-giving destination. Leaders can create and maintain good systems
for becoming and remaining organized through technology and
paper-based systems. Disorganized leaders not only find it difficult to handle the detail-oriented dimensions of change, but they
squander the community's trust by failing to follow through on
promises. Similarly, leaders who fail to inform and remind their
constituents of important messages seem unpredictable to those
in their communities. Predictability promotes confidence on the
part of communities that their leader will always be there for them.

When it comes to organization and communication, habits
are everything. A good to-do list, calendar, and time management
skills are musts. We can improve in our capacities along each of
those lines continuously throughout our lives. Systems for reminding ourselves to communicate with others what we are doing
and why all share this attribute: these systems are easy enough to
set up and then to upgrade.

.•3

Emotion

The Role of Emotion in Change Leadership

Chapter 2 delved into the uneasy relationship between reason and the Christian faith. The early Christian church coexisted with a Greek ideal of a mental state where body and mind were separated, with mind dominating over body and controlling emotion. We still use the term "stoic" to describe a flat affect, which is borrowed from those times. In the church's earliest days, some Christians attempted to disembody Jesus, arguing that he was God on earth and thus could not have suffered in body and mind like humans do. Too terrible for them was the idea that God could have put on human form and suffered with us. Gnostic Christianity, the movement associated with this dualistic notion of mind and body, was cut away from the Christian community and called heresy in favor of an incarnational Christianity, where Jesus was known to be both fully human and fully divine.

And yet today's heresy is just as worrisome: those who cannot reconcile mind and body in Christianity, and who opt for a pure-reason approach to making sense of the world, simply leave faith behind. This exploration of the different dynamics at work in change began with reason because reason provides the easiest on-ramp: change leadership via reason is a well-trod path. At the risk of presenting a tautological argument, reason makes sense. Emotion is less predictable. Its causes and effects are nonlinear, and actions and reactions are shaped by many forces other than what might meet the eye.

Emotions in Daily Living

Jesus had emotions. He expressed joy, sadness, fear, dread, affection, and anger. He also was calm and detached when the occasion called for him to be. He doodled on the ground when a woman's life was at stake. He conversed obliquely with Pilate about whether he deserved to be put to death. He taught his disciples lessons on occasions when it would have been entirely understandable if he had lashed out at them. Jesus's management of his emotions provides what is perhaps an impossible standard in our lives, but one to which we can aspire: where we have emotions, but emotions do not have us. This chapter addresses how emotion shapes change in institutions made up of people and how emotional connection is part of the goal.

When my spouse and I adopted our child, we participated in a series of parenting classes required by the social services agency assessing our readiness for adoption. One of the classes stands out in my mind. I remember the teacher had adopted one or more children from Russia, and in those years many orphaned children from Russia suffered from fetal alcohol syndrome. In the class, I learned that some of these children need extra help in attaching to others, and one of the ways adults could support them was by giving them words to describe their feelings. The four key words we learned in our class—which I have since learned are standbys for counselors of all kinds—were mad, sad, glad, and afraid.

Over the years, I have found that this observation about human attachment is applicable well beyond the context of international adoption. Many adults—and on occasion I count myself among them—have difficulty finding words to describe their emotions, and in those moments, connecting with others can be difficult. We act out rather than describing our feelings and seeking to learn the feelings of others. Instead of coming to terms with our own emotions, we try to control the emotions of those around us. Many parents seek to soothe their irate toddlers with the expression, "Use your words." Words in those cases being better alternatives to hitting, throwing a tantrum, or throwing a bowl of unsatisfactory food on the floor. How many times have I in meetings wanted to tell a participant whose body language was expressing a strong desire not to be present to use her words? Or the student who was disappearing from discussion rather than taking responsibility for their discomfort? Or the parishioner yes-yessing the minister to his face and then undermining him in the parking lot? Using our words is a skill for a lifetime.

Emotions in Community

The emotions held by individuals—gracefully or disappointingly—are not the focus of this chapter. Instead, because leadership and change make up the framework in which this theory is unfolding, the focus will be on emotional systems. This chapter will rely heavily on the work of Edwin Friedman,[37] a rabbi in a Jewish congregation and a counselor to individuals and families whose work took place during the latter part of the twentieth century. We can see connections between his reasoning and the earliest days of the Christian Church, not just Gnostic "heresy" as already described, but also the writings of the Apostle Paul, who was strongly influenced by the Stoics.

In a sermon preached on April 27, 2018, in Marquand Chapel at Yale Divinity School, New Testament professor and Presbyterian minister Michal Beth Dinkler described the way in which Stoicism echoes in today's Christianity. She focused her sermon on Philippians 4:11–12, which reads,

> Not that I am referring to being in need; for I have learned
> to be content with whatever I have. I know what it is to

---

[37] Edwin Friedman, *Generation to Generation: Family Process in Church and Synagogue* (New York: Guilford Press, 1985).

have little, and I know what it is to have plenty. In any and all circumstances I have learned the secret of being well-fed and of going hungry, of having plenty and of being in need.

Dinkler spoke of her difficulty with a passage where Paul sounds as though he is admonishing those who are suffering to accept their situations. Dinkler reconciles the passage with a justice-oriented message by considering it in light of the times, where a Stoic mindset was considered admirable and educated. Dinkler stated:

> The Stoics taught that self-sufficiency comes from rigorously training the self to detach from emotion and relationship. [We still use the adjective "stoic" in that way today.] Paul says he's learned the "secret" [a "secret" he's been blabbing all over the Mediterranean] that self-sufficiency comes not from ourselves, but from the God who gives us strength.

Friedman writes that the appropriate leadership stance in the midst of complex emotional systems is separate-yet-togetherness.[38] Leaders must take responsibility for their own emotions and take good enough care of themselves that they can remain connected, rather than reactively lashing out or detaching. Almost two millennia earlier, we can find in Paul's letters a nuanced stance: we stay separate-yet-connected by relying on God. We build our faith on the rock of God's love, Jesus's teachings, and the hope we find in Jesus's resurrection. For that reason, we need not build our faith on individuals or communities that are sometimes controlled by forces the body's members themselves do not understand. Self-sufficiency is not our purpose; it is God-sufficiency that helps us to find both healthy detachment and real community through a combination of self-love and love for neighbor.

---

[38] Edwin Friedman, *Generation to Generation: Family Process in Church and Synagogue* (New York: Guilford Press, 1985).

In order to ground Friedman's recommended emotional leadership stance—separate-yet-togetherness—in the theory from which it emerges, what will follow is a primer on emotional systems theory.

Emotional Systems Theory

Rabbi Edwin Friedman trained in marriage and family counseling at a time when Bowen family systems theory was making its way through the counseling disciplines. Family systems theory presented a new way of working with clients, considering them not just as individuals who could be separated from a family unit and "cured," but rather as participants in a whole system that needed treatment. I have found the easiest way to describe family systems theory is with the example of a counseling session led by one trained in the method. Bobby is a teenager suffering from addiction. His parents seek out a therapist to help Bobby. The therapist invites Bobby, his parents, and his two siblings to the first session. In the therapist's notes, we see the identifiers for each participant in the conversation labeled "P1, P2, P3, P4," and "IP." "IP" stands for the "identified patient," Bobby, but the whole family is in treatment.

Rabbi Edwin Friedman adapted Bowen family systems theory for use in faith communities. Even the most businesslike congregations refer to themselves, for better or worse, as families. This past Sunday, my spouse and I joined a church in the city to which we have recently moved, and the number of times we were invited and welcomed using family language struck me: I felt like a guest at my own wedding, where both my spouse and I were the new in-laws. Some might say that it is useful to avoid family language for congregations, and that emphasizing the way in which congregations are like families might lead to unhealthy codependence and unrealistic expectations. My opinion: those tendencies exist anyway, named or unnamed, and leaders do better to accept the reality that families and faith communities are similar and, similarly, can be healthy or unhealthy. Families and churches both can become healthier with wise leadership.

A Systems Theory Overview

When I read Friedman for the first time while serving in a dysfunctional office setting and also working part-time at an emotionally complicated church, it shocked me how quickly I revised my understanding of what was taking place around me. Before reading Friedman, I believed—unconsciously but firmly—that all the acting out, opting out, and manipulation I was experiencing in those settings related to choices on the part of individuals. I came to realize that each was playing a role in a system much bigger and stronger than any one person, including myself. Similarly, I went from viewing my own behavior as choices to role-playing in a bigger drama: role-playing from which I could choose to refrain. I learned to ask, "How might I be contributing to this dysfunction?" rather than, "Why is everyone around me so wrong, when I am so right?"

Over the years that I have taught seminary students about leadership, I have found great satisfaction in hearing students describe how family systems theory shifted their consciousness in remarkable ways. For their use and understanding, I have developed a list of key concepts from systems theory, derived from a combination of Friedman and of life experiences where Friedman's ideas have been a help to me:

1. Emotional triangles
2. Homeostasis
3. Walls have memory
4. Identified patient
5. Self-differentiation
6. The fallacy of empathy

7. Emotional blackmail

8. Sabotage is real

I hope the reader's experience of this list is the same: eye-opening, helpful, and bringing a new layer of complexity to the ways in which we experience each other in communities.

Triangulation. In quantitative (studying numbers) and qualitative (studying words) research, triangulation is good. When the data tell us something surprising or exciting, it is ethical and right to triangulate those numbers with another source of data in order to ensure the validity of our findings. In human relationships, some say that triangulation, or the creation of emotional triangles, is bad and wrong. In truth, emotional triangles just are. Any time people are together, relationships move in patterns more complicated than one-on-one. Sometimes, emotional triangles are healthy. Quite often, they cause harm to individuals and dysfunction in the system. Here is how they work:

Betty and Trevor are colleagues in an office setting. Li is Betty's administrative assistant, and Trevor has a different assistant—Andrew—who is not particularly competent. Trevor has sought to discipline or terminate Andrew, but the process has been slow and frustrating. He occasionally groans loudly when talking with Betty about projects that are getting behind schedule, and Li can hear his frustration. Li goes to Trevor to offer assistance without consulting with Betty. She ends up with more work than she can handle, and her effectiveness in assisting Betty suffers. Outward signals would suggest that Andrew's effectiveness is improving, as Trevor's deadlines are met, and Trevor seems happier and more relaxed. He has backed off on plans to terminate Andrew.

In this scenario, Trevor and Andrew's working relationship has become dysfunctional, and Trevor—perhaps unwittingly—has triangulated Li (Figure 3.1). By doing so, pressure comes off of both him and Andrew, but falls on Li's shoulders. Li becomes what is

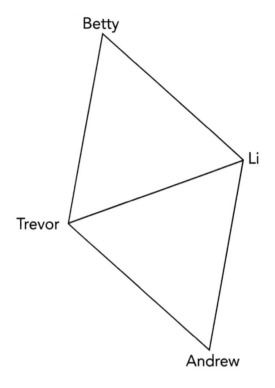

FIGURE 3.1

called in family systems theory the symptom-bearer. Li is likely to become less effective, feel less satisfied at work, and perhaps will develop a stress-related illness. Li is not the one in the position of power in this scenario, and therefore Li is unlikely to be able to change the dynamic. What must Li do? With the assistance of Betty, they both need to put responsibility back where it belongs.

Betty could go to Trevor and explain that Li offered out of a generosity of spirit and a desire to serve, but by taking work off of Andrew's plate, Li is enabling a dysfunctional situation to last longer and do more damage. Betty can explain to Trevor that Li's work is suffering, as is Li. Betty could work with Trevor to create a strategy whereby Li can offer some help during the time it takes to intervene

regarding Andrew's performance, but otherwise, Andrew's responsibilities need to be Andrew's.

De-triangulating is the simple-sounding, but difficult to implement, process of reassigning responsibilities to those who have
the power to carry out those responsibilities. A system in need
of change is one where roles, responsibilities, and power to carry
out action are misaligned and thus fundamentally doomed to fail.
Like an old house onto which room after room has been added,
historic institutions are notorious for such misalignment, as those
with power and those with responsibility might find themselves
separated by several corridors.

De-triangulating by reassigning responsibility to those who
have power to carry it out is particularly difficult in mission-driven
organizations. How many times have I been coached by those
who care about me to let an initiative die on the vine rather than
bailing a colleague out? How many times have I swooped in to
rescue an event whose failure might have harmed not the planner
of the event but the attendees or honorees for whom the event was
intended? We have all done it and—who am I kidding?—others
have done it for me. We cannot de-triangulate out of spite, and
we cannot allow those we serve (including our organizations) to
suffer because a team member was not firing on all cylinders. In
missional organizations, we do not have the easy out of telling
ourselves we are not getting paid for others' work; we were not
getting paid very much in the first place.

De-triangulating is not about being unhelpful. Rather, we
de-triangulate so as to heal sick systems and in the interest of protecting the symptom-bearer of such sick systems over the long
haul. We also de-triangulate in order to avoid enabling unhealthy
systems to endure needlessly, unconfronted and thus replicated.

Homeostasis. Just as water seeks its own level and people's fun-
damental personalities tend to remain fixed, organizations—such as

families and churches—establish and seek homeostasis as a means of preserving their communal senses of identity. "Homeo" means same, and "stasis" means status or situation. Systems seek to preserve that which is, even when it does not serve the collective good. Religious communities are particularly prone to sustaining an insufficient homeostasis for protracted periods of time, sometimes until they run out of money or people or both. I believe that one reason this tends to happen is that religious organizations cherish tradition and exist in part to relay that tradition from one generation to another. Understanding the difference between a life-giving tradition and a change-fearing equilibrium requires wisdom and perspective.

Like triangulation, homeostasis is neither good nor bad, inherently. It is the state of affairs, the reality, the closest thing to what an organization could call normal. A healthy homeostasis versus an unhealthy one? That is the only real question. Sometimes students of systems theory confuse homeostasis with being stuck, but actually, some institutions normalize innovation and progress and are unable to feel like themselves if things stay the same for too long.

In the political climate in which I write, the president of the United States is most appreciated by those who claim to want to shake up Washington, D.C., and break down structures of power that are no longer, to their minds, serving the nation. What I see is a president who promotes disequilibrium with no sense of direction toward a more satisfying homeostasis. He shakes things up by keeping people confused and feeling insecure. He uses unpredictability to keep the upper hand, not to reach toward a new goal. I predict that this style of leadership will be ultimately unhelpful in bringing the country together around a shared vision, were that ever the intent. People are willing to tolerate a great deal of disruption if a higher purpose might be gained. I fear chaos will continue to reign and is already becoming a new normal.

A few months ago, when persons brought to the country illegally by their parents as children were threatened with deportation, I wrote an email to the students I serve, reassuring them that if they were undocumented, we would stick up for them. Tensions were running so high that I felt it might help our students to focus on their studies if they knew someone would have their back at this confusing moment.

I also wanted to make a point to students about leadership: keeping those who were vulnerable guessing, turning them against each other, and not allowing them to make their plans or even process their feelings is destructively bad leadership. Homeostasis is not the enemy; it is a state of being that gives institutions and communities needed internal coherence. When homeostasis is threatened by disequilibrium, with no plan in sight, the organization will strive to restore even the worst attributes of homeostasis rather than face chaos and rudderlessness. It is for this reason that wise leadership is most needed during and after times of disruption so that the new homeostasis might be healthier than the one that came before, recognizing that homeostasis will, by its very nature, reinstitute itself if it can.

Walls have memory. Related to the concept of homeostasis is the notion that emotional triangles and homeostasis endure irrespective of the cast of characters. Friedman calls his book on family systems theory *Generation to Generation* for a reason: institutions and communities shape their inhabitants as much as, or perhaps even more than, people shape their communities and institutions. Patterns of behavior can endure over surprising lengths of time, despite other changes internal and external to the community.

When teaching a course on ministerial leadership in historic faith communities, I assigned students a project in which they considered a change in a ministry setting. One student decided to study the history behind a position that had been created for him in a

church, where he was going to be among the first paid professional religious educators to run the Sunday school. He was stunned
to learn that the idea of having a professional religious educator,
rather than solely volunteers in the role, was anything but new. The
church had lived through controversy after controversy throughout
its 300-year history as to the responsibility of clergy for the religious education of children. Three centuries of the same pattern!
This knowledge helped the student to understand that he had been
brought in to solve a problem whose roots were deeper than anyone
in the congregation knew besides him. His knowledge would not be
enough to get this tension out of the system, but awareness helped
him not to underestimate the challenge before him.

Of course, 300-year-old controversies are rare. Less rare is the
way in which dysfunction tends to replicate itself in the service of
protecting homeostasis. Most religious leaders can think of an example of a time when they were relieved when a dysfunctional family left
the faith community, only to find that family replaced: a new family
arrived or a longstanding family's behavior changed and replaced the
dysfunction. Unless the minister addresses the dysfunction, one person who leaves after questioning every leadership decision is bound
to have a successor.

Unaddressed problems do not go away just because individuals move on. Last summer when my school was relocating, I
was responsible for deciding which faculty personnel records to
keep and which to shred, and I saw many documents I had not
read previously. I found myself laughing out loud repeatedly as I
learned of old controversies that, but for the names, were exactly
like those I had experienced in recent years. I read correspondence
from a faculty member who had left the school fifty years before
I had arrived whose concerns were so similar to those of a current
faculty member that I could have interchanged the files.

Much like homeostasis, that history repeats itself is neither good nor bad. It is simply a dimension of being part of an emotional system, which all communities are. Ensuring that destructive history stays in the past is the leadership challenge, and part of dismantling dysfunction so it cannot repeat itself requires understanding this: just because a dysfunctional person has gone away does not mean that the dysfunction itself will be put to bed. When Larry Nasser, the abusive doctor to the USA Women's Olympic Gymnastics Team, was finally held accountable, it would have been easy for those affected to breathe a sigh of relief to see him placed behind bars for life. Those who were wiser to the dynamics of systems recognized that it was the system that gave Nasser access to those who were vulnerable, and it was the system that would need to change if trust were to be restored. Those who underestimate the power of systems—thinking they are smarter than the system is strong—are the ultimate enablers of the dysfunctional actors in communities.

Identified patient. I previously used the concept of the "identified patient" to illustrate how family systems therapy might differ from an individualistic psychotherapeutic model. In institutional leadership as opposed to psychotherapy, the concept changes only slightly in implementation. The concept of the identified patient in a faith community or religious organization lays bare our tendencies to oversimplify conflict and to scapegoat agitators. Can you think of an example where you, in your leadership role, were warned about someone in the community? "This person is a real problem," you might have heard; "she is out to get you." Only the naïve leader takes those warnings at face value. Those the community chooses to single out as problems tell us more about the community than about any one individual. As was described in the preceding section on homeostasis, bad actors are playing a role. Sometimes they are genuinely toxic, and other times they are the symptom-bearers of a sick system.

How can leaders treat the whole system rather than focusing all of our energies and anxieties on the identified patient? First, we can keep in perspective our "if-only" fantasies. One of my favorite cynical jokes about ministry—among many I have stored up over the years—is this: "Pastoral ministry would be the perfect job if we could just kill one a year." Fantasies are illusions in our mind that if one difficult person would simply go away, everything would be better. A systems perspective would indicate that the person we fantasize disappearing will be immediately replaced. We must find ways to cope in the here and now, recognizing that the bad actor might be part toxic and part playing out a role in the system.

Second, we can decide where to place our energies, sending more of our time and attention to those whose gifts and whose needs are adding life to the community, and less time and attention to those who are draining the community of energy. Martin Copenhaver has taught me more about the importance of considering the source than any other person. He does not pay attention to anonymous feedback. He listens to criticism but takes it most seriously when it comes from those he respects.

Third, and relatedly, we can use a systems approach rather than zeroing in on one person as the "problem child." In a community where one person is wreaking havoc, we have to ask: How could the organization be set up in such a way that it can be disrupted so completely by one person? If the identified patient is among the leaders, we can ask: How is it that we empowered a person into leadership who has toxic tendencies? How might we cultivate leaders who are a force for the good, and how might we support and nurture future leaders who are ready to bring health to a team?

Self-differentiation. Few concepts from systems theory are more universally relevant to life, love, and leadership than self-differentiation. The idea is simple: knowing where you end and others begin is essential to being in relationship with other people. Living out self-differentiation is the project of a lifetime. Many who feel called to serve in mission-driven organizations care deeply about others. Some come from codependent backgrounds, with families of origin where the boundaries were blurry or nonexistent. The greatest gift a person can bring to service is a deep sense of connection with others. The greatest liability can be difficulty separating the needs of others from our own wants, needs, and goals.

In his last book, *A Failure of Nerve*,[39] Friedman writes: focus on your own emotions. When I have assigned this book to seminary students, their reactions to this idea have at times been strongly negative, as they have been taught that self-focus is selfish. In such cases, I have assigned an experiment: next time you find yourself in an emotionally complicated conversation, stop trying to read the person to whom you are speaking, and instead focus on your own feelings. What is happening in your body? What thoughts are intruding upon you? Quite often, the results have been positive. The ones who have vehemently resisted the idea of a self-focus have found that the person with whom they were speaking eased up and relaxed almost immediately in the presence of a person who was engaging in emotional self-management. When we think in a self-differentiated way, it shows on our faces and in our words. When we are not trying to manage the emotions of others, they begin to take responsibility for their own emotions, just as we do for ourselves. Uncanny, truly. Yet, with all these benefits, why is self-differentiation so difficult to sustain?

When we are among those who care, we experience pain when unhappiness surrounds us. When we try to manage the emotions of others, we are on a fool's errand, but even if we know that, stopping is difficult. Self-differentiation is not an event; it is a process. We cultivate it over years, and thankfully we can improve in self-differentiating as we mature as people and leaders. One of the

---

39 Friedman, *A Failure of Nerve*.

costs of improvement in self-differentiation is that those around us might find us cold if we suddenly seem unaffected by their plights. In my experience, women in particular are expected to respond with compassion to the emotions of others, at all times and in all places. When those we lead are disappointed that their upset does not seem to unmoor us, they might label us cold or uncaring. For clergy of all genders, the expectation that ministers will change their behavior based on the turmoil they sense is a workplace hazard. Friedman writes that a leader occasionally described as "cold" should consider it a compliment.

How do we improve in our self-differentiation? For Friedman, the ideal self-differentiated stance for a leader is separate-yet-connected. The leader knows her own goals and opinions but can hear and become influenced by the ideas of others. She cares when those she serves are upset, but she does not go along for the ride. None of us is good at this all the time. We tend to regress with our families of origin or with people we have known through various phases of our lives. But practices of cultivating self-differentiation, such as spiritual and physical health, therapy that gives us perspective, and friendships with healthy others are worthy of our time and disciplined attention.

The fallacy of empathy. Less popular still with seminary students, but recognizably helpful for religious leaders serving communities, is the idea that empathy is not a worthy goal toward which leaders should strive. Empathy, according to Friedman, can be a tool of manipulation used by communities to undermine leaders. The idea—Friedman would say the faulty premise—behind empathy relates to human understanding. When we say we can empathize with another, we suggest that we can feel their pain or at least relate to it. A leader who lacks empathy makes choices that affect others without thinking about the impact of those choices. Certainly, those with power must discipline themselves to be considerate of those over whom they have power, but this does not mean they can perfectly imagine what those over whom they have power are feeling.

The leadership stance that takes the fallacy of empathy seriously comes across like this: "I do not pretend to understand you. I know that you are not me, but rather a separate person with your own hopes and problems. I am ready to listen to you." When we claim to have empathy, we misuse our power in that we project the feelings we expect onto another without truly listening. Just recently, I had a conversation with a person who has power over me. That person made an assumption that something was important to me, and the assumption was incorrect. That leader was trying to demonstrate empathy, but the strategy backfired: I felt invisible and unknown. I would have liked so much more to have been asked. Curiosity trumps empathy as a leadership posture in virtually every case.

Emotional blackmail. Those who work amidst group dynamics daily know that reactivity—lashing out when overcome with emotion—is not just for toddlers. Adults pout. Senior citizens have tantrums. Seasoned professionals threaten to take their buckets and shovels and go play in another sandbox when they do not get their way. In faith communities, harmonious interpersonal dynamics are not just preferable but paramount. Therefore, those who want their way can take advantage of this hunger for harmony in order to get it. They can create disharmony so as to get their needs met. Reactivity is the opposite of what was described previous as separate-yet-togetherness. Whether in the form of explosiveness, withdrawal, or threats, individuals within the system behave reactively out of a lack of self-differentiation.

In his book *Exit, Voice, and Loyalty,*[40] Orin Hirschman writes that we have choices when we are part of an organization or society moving in what we consider to be a wrong direction: we can opt

---

[40] Albert O. Hirschman, *Exit, Voice, and Loyalty: Responses to Decline in Firms, Organizations, and States* (Cambridge, MA: Harvard University Press, 1970).

out, speak up, or stay true to those with authority. Reactivity is not a meaningful option. It does not involve a choice to do anything, but rather it is the tool of the emotional blackmailer seeking to take advantage of the community's hopes for togetherness. Those who hold the community hostage by reactivity usually do so in a calculating way, whether they admit it to themselves or not. Rarely does a leader storm out of a meeting in anger, except with the hope someone will chase him or her out and beg for forgiveness. Rarely does a member of a community fold their arms over their chest glowering rather than speaking up, except when hoping someone will ask, "What is wrong?"

When a group is in an emotional hostage situation, the self-differentiated leader can model a separate-yet-together way of engaging the hijacker. We can call the hostage-taker out: "Your body language suggests you're upset, Jules. Would you like to say a word at this point, or are you still formulating your thoughts?" We can model to others in the community how to find harmony amidst reactivity: "I am sorry that C. J. felt they couldn't stay in the meeting due to the tension we are all experiencing; let's pray for them . . . and now let's continue." Allowing the blackmailer to reset or scuttle an agenda is almost always the wrong thing for a leader to do.

Sabotage is real. Painful as it is for leaders to admit, some individuals within the emotional system will want the change effort to fail. This reality is hard to accept because it is so illogical and disappointing. Conversely, some agitators for change in community, who want what is truly best for the mission of the organization, are labeled incorrectly and unfairly as saboteurs. The real causes for concern are, or should be, those whose inner lives are tumultuous and full of pain and who seek to cause the communities in their lives to become just as tumultuous and painful in order to find affirmation and equilibrium.

I offered consultation to a new church start some years ago

where the leadership was in conflict. As the church had grown and become increasingly successful, the lay leaders started beating up on the clergy. The bullies' tactics were reminiscent of bullies on a playground going after the kids who seemed overly happy and well-liked; the behavior was just as immature. I observed that the leaders in the new church start had all left more traditional faith communities, having been hurt. I observed that, as the new church started to take on more of the trappings of a traditional congregation, the lay leaders were having bad memories. They were unwittingly sabotaging the new church in order to reaffirm their reasons for leaving their past communities. Their unresolved anger was creating a mess inside some of the leaders, and they were subconsciously creating a mess outside them to match.

Emotion-Based Change Leadership Strategies and Practices

Sick systems can be fixed and are in fact improved every day, just not in the way leaders sometimes think. In the last chapter, I proposed that a reason-based leadership stance includes teaching and planning as the primary activities. An emotions-based leadership stance includes (1) embodying self-differentiation and nonanxiety; (2) aligning authority, placing responsibility where it belongs; and (3) respecting that emotional systems are strong: stronger than individuals, stronger than reason, and not to be underestimated.

Embodying Self-Differentiation

Self-differentiation, and its outward expression as a nonanxious presence, is the hallmark of a leader who understands emotional systems. The nonanxious presence requires much more than an affect of calm; Botox could accomplish that. A nonanxious presence requires an inner sense of boundaries between members of a community: permeable and healthy. The nonanxious presence exemplifies self-differentiation, and those around the nonanxious presence are reminded that they too have whole selves from which they could be engaging others.

Potential obstacles to effective leadership through self-differentiation and a nonanxious presence include the discouragement that comes with regular setbacks and the fear some of us have of being perceived as uncaring. Setbacks are normal. As mentioned previously, no one is nonanxious all the time, and no one is self-differentiated on every front in their lives. The institutional leader who is the picture of equanimity at work might be the picture of codependence at home. The day we feel like we have finally created a healthy boundary between ourselves and those who have power over us might be the same day we hide in a closet to cry after a rough meeting. Cultivating nonanxiety is like any other form of practice, which means sometimes we take two steps forward and one step back.

Also described previously, fear of being perceived as one who does not care is particularly acute for leaders who are women and leaders in institutions whose missions include ministries of care. After years of experimenting with nonanxiety as a leadership practice, I have become a believer. I am not successful at it all the time, by any means. A friend recently told me that he can read my attempted poker face as well as any other facial expression. I will always have to keep my own anxiety in check, and I tend to be an expressive person. These are parts of who I am, and authenticity matters too, but I try to keep my anxiety . . . mine.

For religious leaders, faith practices are one necessary basis for a sustained nonanxious presence. When we cultivate a deep Christian faith, we build our nonanxiety on a solid foundation: Christ has died, Christ was risen, Christ will come again; what have we to fear? Meditative prayer practices help leaders to detach helpfully at certain times of day, reminding themselves how to do that. Praying for help from God to stay calm and grounded in the midst of tension is another way in which we plant our feet onto solid ground rather than the shifting sands of emotional systems. Weekly worship, daily prayer and meditation, spiritual retreats and direction, faith-filled friendships, and constant learning about God's activity in the world all help us to embody constancy amidst turmoil.

Perhaps the most obvious, and therefore most commonly forgotten, dimension of embodying self-differentiation is the practice of having a life. We are *part* of communities; communities do not and cannot define us. We have our ministries, our jobs, our families, our hobbies, our guilty pleasures, our virtuous pleasures, our pets, our homes, our fitness routines, our vacation plans—and no one of those things can be the sole source of our identities. Why? Because any one of those things could become troubled and fall through. Only God is a solid foundation, and, beyond God, we must diversify our emotional portfolios.

Aligning Authority: Putting Responsibility Where It Belongs

The second leadership practice for one who appreciates emotional systems theory is structural in nature: when we have the power to do so, we should align power with responsibility. Then we should do all we can to avoid emotional triangles that seek to place responsibility on those who do not have adequate power to carry it. These two steps *should* go together, but in reality do so only rarely. Amidst complex emotional systems, boundaries become unclear. We hold people responsible for that which they cannot control, and we find ourselves confused about that for which we are responsible.

Consider this example: in my denomination, the United Church of Christ, judicatory leaders often find themselves frustrated because they are held responsible for the well-being of churches over whose decisions they have no authority. It is my conviction that this is a structural issue that will only improve when responsibility and power are more closely aligned, where judicatory leaders are not held responsible for that which they cannot control or are given authority to control more. Suspicion about centralized power is behind our denomination's reluctance to make such structural changes; that suspicion exemplifies the concepts of the walls having memory. Holding a leader responsible without giving them power to carry out responsibilities is not just demoralizing; it is bad for the overall health of the organization.

Consider another example: No Child Left Behind, an education policy initiative in the early 2000s, held teachers accountable for student achievement. This despite the fact that educational research had long shown that teachers are just one of many actors who influence student achievement. Stable parents, reliable housing, and nutrition play roles as significant as instruction in student testing. The policy rolled out undeterred by common sense. The field of educational research has never been the same, as teachers now understandably suspect that data may be used against them. We still call a school and its teachers "good" or "bad" depending on their students' test scores. The goal a leader should have in assigning power, and holding those we lead accountable, should be in alignment.

When that alignment has been achieved, a leader must keep placing responsibility where it belongs. Of course, leaders at times must take quasi-symbolic responsibility for mistakes that were not their own. When a junior staff person makes a major blunder that the leader should have caught or prevented, the senior leader should chastise the staff person privately and take public responsibility for the error. In most cases, putting responsibility where it belongs after structures are aligned properly is less public and more subtle.

When a person behaves reactively—blowing up in or sulking through a meeting, for instance—that person must not be rescued.

Only they can control their behavior, and when they attempt to use or control others, they must either be ignored or called out on the carpet. They can be taught to express themselves more helpfully, using words like, "I disagree," and phrases like, "I don't like the direction we're taking here." The best way we can teach people to take responsibility for what they control (say, their behavior), and let go of responsibility for what we cannot control (such as the behavior of others), is modeling separate-yet-togetherness through a nonanxious presence.

Boundaries are the way in which leaders construct internal and external systems for keeping power and responsibility where they belong. Cultivating healthy boundaries is a way to take care of others and take responsibility for ourselves. In the most generalized shorthand, we manage boundaries by remembering whom we are to serve, and by whom we are served, and not mixing those roles up. When we use people, or let them use us, we cultivate unwellness not just in our lives but in our communities. In my faith tradition, the United Church of Christ, ministers must undergo boundary awareness training regularly in order to maintain their ordained standing. Some resent that this training has to be completed often, rather than just once, but I am grateful for the expectation. We lose track of our boundaries in the same way we get drawn into emotional systems: gradually, and when we are least expecting it.

Respecting Systems

Finally, an effective leadership strategy amidst emotional systems is to respect them for their strength as well as their stubbornness. When you meet a religious leader who has been in a role for six months to a year, and she claims that she has changed the system in her setting, make a mental note to circle back with her later when she experiences a painful surprise. Systems do not change quickly, if they change at all. The two leadership practices just described—self-differentiation and placing responsibility and power in proximity to one another—can help a system to become healthier over time. They can also help the leader in the system to endure in leadership long enough for real change to emerge. Two separate but related concepts help us to understand why systems are sometimes stronger than leaders: schemata and burnout.

First, the adult brain follows engrained patterns known as schemata. Schemata, plural for schema or scheme, are the shortcuts our mind builds over the course of our lives to make sense of the world around us. As children, we experience new sensory information with wonder: it is all new to us. Over time, as we receive the same sensory information repeatedly or routinely, our brain puts it into a category for the sake of efficiency. We experience our first raindrops as a miracle falling from the sky. Later, we see raindrops on our windshield and turn on the wipers without giving the matter another thought; it is just rain, after all.

Adult education scholars attest that schemata can be so strong as to render useless attempts to dislodge unhelpful ones. For instance, the adult learner who has been told he is a bad student his whole life but wants to learn a new trade might never fully believe his successes are real. The educator must meet that learner where the learner is at and foster discovery rather than expecting the schemata to change. Schemata change from shortcuts to neural pathways over time and become hard-wired into adult cognition. Systems and schemata follow the same formula: they do not go away, but they can be rerouted in healthier directions. We are wise to take a lesson from adult educators who respect schemata and educate adults with them in mind, rather than pretending that the adult brain can be somehow turned back into the brain of a child.

Second, burnout is the price to be paid by a leader who fails to respect that systems are stronger than any one leader is smart, gifted, or even right. Oft misunderstood as the result of working too hard,

burnout is a form of emotional exhaustion and depression that results from laboring in a context of insufficient resources, in such a
way that the leader is doomed to fail. A leader becomes burned out
not from long hours, but from working under unrealistic expectations set by others or themselves. When responsibility and power are
insufficiently proximate in the work environment, burnout is possible. When the leader does not believe the emotional systems to have
power—even ultimate power—over how effective or ineffective an
effort at change might be, burnout is all but inevitable. The best
idea in the world could languish because of a system's determination
to maintain an ineffective homeostasis. The leader who thinks that
they can rail and prevail against the system is bound to use up their
energy before an initiative is even off the ground.

The leader who works within the system—understanding that
schemata govern collective thought patterns and avoiding burnout
by setting realistic expectations—can make small and thoughtful
adjustments that take systems seriously without allowing them to
prevent meaningful and important ministry to take place. I have
written elsewhere about the strategies "isomorphism"[41] and "counterweighting."[42] Isomorphism, whose root words are "iso" as in
same, and "morphism" as in shape, is a tactic whereby the leader
makes something new look familiar. Counterweighting is similar,
in that we offset change in one area of an organization with sustaining tradition in another area. Just as these strategies help give
those we lead change at a tolerable rate, they also make it possible to bring about change without needlessly upsetting the emotional system. We must budget our energies to prevent burnout.

Here is an example: I served a campus ministry center that
had fallen on hard times. I was called to either turn the ministry

---

[41] Jackson W. Carroll, *God's Potters: Pastoral Leadership and the Shaping of Congregations*
(Grand Rapids, MI: Eerdmans, 2006).

[42] L. Gregory Jones and Kevin R. Armstrong, *Resurrecting Excellence: Shaping Faithful Christian
Ministry* (Grand Rapids, MI: Eerdmans, 2006).

around or shut it down. The sign on the exterior of the building was hand-painted, unprofessional, and looked nothing like any other sign on campus, although it faced the student union. The sign proclaimed by its ragtag appearance, "This place is 'other,' and that is the role of religion on this campus." I pulled the sign down with a crow bar on my first day of work. I partnered with students in choosing a new logo—one of the students designed it, in fact—and raised money from a local church to buy a new sign. Our grant proposal to the church was entitled, "We are looking for a sign from God." The name was the same but the logo was new. Those two traits balanced each other out. The font on the sign was the same as those on buildings in the wider university.

Although they must disrupt the emotional system with care, leaders have to do it. A certain amount of regular innovation is crucial for institutional survival. In property management, the term we identify to describe this phenomenon is "deferred maintenance." Smart institutions set aside enough money for capital improvements every year so that they can undergo a full renovation every ten or twenty. Wise institutional leaders do the same with programs, policies, and practices. They hold onto enough energy every year to seriously consider their effectiveness, and every few seasons they take time to consider a comprehensive review and possible restructuring. That ongoing evaluation and occasional jubilee are what I call leadership maintenance, which is deferred only by the unwise.

Self-differentiation and a nonanxious presence; putting responsibility and power in proximity to one another, and then putting responsibility where it belongs; and respecting the strength of systems are all practices that can help a leader to be effective within even the least healthy emotional systems. Isomorphism and counterweighting, as well as normalizing regular institutional maintenance through evaluation, are specific leadership practices that take systems seriously without giving them the last word.

Emotions and Theology

I began this chapter describing the uneasy relationship between emotion and religion in the early Christian church. I then skipped directly to today, where reason and emotion find themselves locked in political tension. Supporters of President Donald Trump seem not to care when President Trump makes statements that are patently untrue, which defies reason. They are so moved by him emotionally in his salesmanship of ideas that please them that they suspend reason in favor of the way he makes them feel. Conversely, opponents of President Trump continue to hammer away at their reason-based views, failing to connect emotionally while condescending to those who are inspired. Liberals claim to want dialogue but are not able to listen to any positions infused with emotion; they want to reason together, but only on their own terms. I suspect this stalemate will endure far beyond the publication of this book.

Between the time of the early Christian church and today's political deadlock in the United States, two religious movements showed us what can happen when emotion and reason kiss each other: the Jesuit movement within the Roman Catholic Church and the Great Awakenings in New England. The Jesuits were founded by St. Ignatius of Loyola in sixteenth-century France. Although their hallmark was founding institutions of higher learning, their spirituality took emotions seriously. Ignatius paid close attention to his feelings, understanding them to be God's way of communicating with him. The practices of discernment he taught all sought to help individuals and communities to know what they really wanted, using their emotions as a divining rod.

In eighteenth-century in New England, a series of religious revivals brought sleepy Congregational faith to life. Primarily a youth movement at its beginning, the first Great Awakening in New England inspired, and was inspired by, the thinking and writing of Jonathan Edwards. Edwards—a theological hero among mainline and evangelical Christians alike—connected the massive, emotional, Holy Spirit–infused gatherings with Jesus's work on souls in a way that valued both learning and the experience of feeling moved.[43] One hundred years later, it was Edwards' grandson Timothy Dwight who called for a return to lived experience of faith, as opposed to overreliance on reason, during what became the Second Great Awakening. When Dwight imagined Andover Seminary as its inspirer and first convocation speaker, and reimagined Yale University as its president, he envisioned an intellectual clergy that was nonetheless dedicated to conversion expressed through revival spirituality.[44]

In the United Church of Christ today, it is my ardent hope that emotion and reason can work together, with Christ at the meeting point of the two. I fear that reasoning about social justice, and then reasoning about theology, is too much of the same. Without heart, the body has no engine for moving its lifeblood. Heart and head together are what energize faith communities, and leaders must speak to both.

 ## Exercise: Family (Systems) Feud

The following game will help you or a group together to assess how well they have come to understand family systems theory as relates to change leadership in institutions. Consider each scenario and select the response you think best.

Scenario 1. A colleague you respect comes to you to discuss a senior leader in your organization who is "phoning it in" en route to retirement.

> a) You listen sympathetically and offer your colleague the opportunity to come and talk any time.

---

43 George M. Marsden, *A Short Life of Jonathan Edwards* (Grand Rapids, MI: William B. Eerdmans, 2008).

44 Margaret Bendroth, *The Last Puritans: Mainline Protestants and the Power of the Past* (Chapel Hill, NC: University of North Carolina Press, 2015).

b) You change the subject to another work-related issue.

c) You brainstorm with your colleague how they can bring concerns directly to the senior leader.

d) You loyally go to the senior leader yourself to relay concerns, including the concern that people are talking.

Scenario 2. You are part of a selection committee for a scholarship. Candidates and committee members are all different from each other.

a) You study the criteria for the scholarship, and you try to learn as much as you can about the scholarship's history.

b) You insist that the committee create a ranking scale and that the committee has a system for voting.

c) You sit back and allow the process to unfold.

d) You read who on the committee has the most relevant experience and study that person's choices and opinions in forming your own.

Scenario 3. You discover that your predecessor misused your organization's funds and that the board not only knew about the malfeasance but organized a quiet departure rather than holding your predecessor accountable.

a) You make sure that all conduct was legal and then let it go.

b) You make sure that all conduct was legal and ask for a meeting with the board about what happened.

c) You insist that the board go public on the malfeasance, concerned that constituents might scapegoat you otherwise.

d) You ask the board to resign and tell them you will if they won't.

Scenario 4. You receive a letter from a person you do not know who was once involved in your organization. It accuses you of being a bad leader.

a) You write back, "You claim I'm awful. Who knows, you may be right. Want to talk?"

b) You do not write back at all but put the letter in a file for future reference.

c) You touch base with a long-timer at your organization to find out who this person is, and what the person might be looking for.

d) Any of the above.

Scenario 5. During a meeting you are chairing, a participant gets upset and walks out.

a) You name the tension and then resume the agenda. The next day you email the person who walked out with a warm word.

b) You dash out after that person, offer some time for a conversation, and then encourage the person to return.

c) You stay in the room and shift the topic of the meeting to what might be happening that led the person to leave.

d) You bring the meeting to a close, promising to get back in touch once you have figured out what led to such a strong reaction.

Scenario 6. You learn that the organization you serve has a history of getting into financial trouble by planning overly optimistically.

a) You investigate the pattern and find out what need is fulfilled by overpromising and how else that need might be met.

b) You make a promise that you will never let that happen under your leadership.

c) You find out who has been to blame for budgeting overreach and make sure that the person gets set straight or is replaced.

d) Any of the above.

Scenario 7. Every meeting you attend with the elected leaders in the community you serve gets hypergranular, focusing on small details rather than vital matters of sustainability.

a) You suggest a series of "vital questions" meetings for the elected leaders where the subject is the future of the organization.
b) You participate in regular meetings, intentionally dropping relevant seeds into the overly detailed conversations.
c) You stop attending meetings.
d) You consider where else meaningful conversations could take place about sustainability and stoke fires in those settings.

Answer Key

Scenario 1, C. The leadership stances most effective amidst emotional triangles are separate-yet-togetherness and putting responsibility where it belongs. By supporting your colleague by listening with care and encouraging your colleague to go directly to the source of the problems the colleague is experiencing, you are modeling that you care but that you are not going to be a receptacle of venting, nor will you become personally involved in the conflict between two other parties. Separation does not mean distancing, but it is necessary to avoid becoming the symptom-bearer of the sick situation.

Scenario 2, A. The key here is recognizing your role in this situation. You are not the chair of the committee. You should take your role seriously and remember that the walls have memory, and history matters. Published criteria and history are the two main areas to which you must pay attention; you need not overfunction by taking over the process, even when the process is unsatisfactory, which in this case we have no reason to believe it is.

Scenario 3, B. Nonanxiety in cases like these are key; any issue that involves money, malpractice, and lawyers is bound to raise tensions to a fevered pitch if the executive leader is losing their head. The board is responsible for supervising the senior, executive leader. That was someone who misused funds, and now it is you. Three words that should leap to mind when misconduct has been discovered or suggested as a possibility: we must investigate. Only after investigation is there sufficient basis for choosing a next step.

Scenario 4, D. Any of the responses listed could be the right one. Much depends on the tone of the letter, the areas of concern raised, and the emotional triangles in which the letter-writer might be connected. It could very well be that the letter writer is the symptom-bearer of an emotional triangle involving two others with whom you work closely, and that person might need help putting responsibility where it belongs. It could be that the person is chronically angry at the world, and worthy of your prayers but no further attention. A nonanxious state of mind will help you listen to your instincts as to the right response based on the situation.

Scenario 5, A. Do not negotiate with emotional terrorists. Reactivity is often strategic, and although a reactive person would like you to think that she or he was unable to control their behavior, they were. Emotional blackmail is not the sign of an evil person, but rather a person with needs that should be fulfilled in a healthier way. By your continuing with the meeting, but then modeling a better way to get attention by following up with kindness, the hostage-taker does not receive the ransom that would have inevitably led to further acting out.

Scenario 6, A. Respect the strength of the system and know that the walls have memory. By taking seriously that the pattern of living shirtsleeves to shirtsleeves is part of the emotional fabric of the institution, you just might be the one to arrest and reverse the pattern. Thinking that you are smarter than that pattern is a recipe for disappointment. Thinking that one bad apple could be removed and solve the whole problem would only lead to a replacement bad apple next time around.

Scenario 7, D. This scenario, of any of the above, is answered differently from an emotional systems perspective than from the perspective of reason or power. Chances are, I would try steps A and B before D, but a purist of family systems theory would not bother. The purist would rather trust that the system is too strong to get discussion onto another level and would avoid beating their head against a wall. In church turnaround theory, a trusted practice is investing energy into informal spheres of influence where energy serves well, and then migrating that energy over into formal power structures. That is the strategy that would be preferred here by one who cared about family systems theory.

 ## Exercise: Case Study

You are the associate director of a nonprofit that focuses on healthcare for the unhoused. Your portfolio includes connecting with other agencies in your city that care about those who are homeless but have different emphases. Your boss, the executive director, has been an important mentor to you. Her spouse is the executive director of another agency, a relatively new food bank that serves as a clearinghouse for food donations to all the meal programs in the city. Your boss asks you, as a favor, to help her spouse to network with the agencies with whom your agency partners. She suggests taking her spouse with you on a visit to a local elected official. Your boss's spouse takes over the meeting, to which you had brought an ambitious request, and you are left with no time to present your agenda. You leave the meeting empty-handed. Diagram the emotional triangles shaping your dilemma.

Gifts for Change Leadership

An effective leader amidst change is grounded and differentiated. When change is afoot, emotions run hot. A leader who is self-authorizing and calm can do more for keeping the temperature down than the most organized and communicative anxious person. For that reason, groundedness in our faith and our bodies is essential for guiding a community through change to something new and better. Differentiated leaders do not lose their cool when those around them are upset. They can be fully present to others without joining in intense feelings, thus helping the upset person to take responsibility for those emotions.

Whereas organization and communication are about taking on habits, groundedness and differentiation have more to do with letting go. A healthy detachment is best cultivated through practices of wellness. When we are rooted in our bodies and souls, it is easier for us to tell where we end and others begin; the membrane that defines what is ours to handle is discernible to us and to others. I strengthen this membrane with the help of fitness, nutrition, yoga, massage, and regular contact with real friends. Practicing my faith, which is a daily part of my life, reminds me that I am God's child and enmeshed in God's love, nothing else.

.•4

Power

The Role of Power in Change Leadership

As I begin this chapter, I am three years into a process that has led my small, historic, struggling seminary to merge with a strong, world-class university divinity school. Power is never far from my mind. I personally have gone from being a big fish in a small pond to a small fish in what feels like an ocean—not all bad, but challenging. I have had to ask permission to conduct administrative tasks I had carried out autonomously for more than a decade. I am moving from a role as a one-person band to an actor in a large, complex machine. My institution is going through a version of the same transition. The base is stronger because we are now part of a powerful whole. The attendant identity shifts surprise me on a daily basis. I had no idea how liberating it would be to have so much less responsibility, especially responsibility for that which I could not control. I had no idea my ego could be bruised by those from whom I expected no fealty nor deference.

In the theoretical framework on which hangs the structure of this book, power is at the bottom, but at the widest part of the triangle, for a reason. It is far from the terrain where leadership takes place, not because it does not influence that terrain, but because of its very elusiveness. Well-meaning, God-serving institutions do not embrace conversation about power; many would like to think that they do not even have any. In its very nature—its chemistry? its physics?—power knows that its exposure could lead to its oblivion. Power is like a cockroach: when the lights go on, it skitters out of sight.

Because of the elusive nature of power, it falls to those with power to reflect honestly on power's nature and effects. Why those with power? Because oppressors, writes Brazilian liberationist educator Paolo Freire, must be liberated along with those over whom they have power.[45] Oppression is unidirectional: those with power impose it on those they oppress. The oppressed dream of having that power, and when they find it, they become oppressors, and oppression endures.

No one likes to think of themselves as an oppressor. No one likes to think of themselves as the oppressed. In fact, no one is oppressor or oppressed in every part of life. Each of us has power over some people and not others, influence in some settings but not all, control over certain resources but not every resource needed to accomplish our goals. Because we do not have power over everything, we often deceive ourselves into thinking we do not have power over anything. And when we do, we are more likely to abuse our power for lack of self-examination on how to use it well. Therefore, in this chapter's examination of leadership, change, and power, we begin with a self-analysis exercise to promote reflection on the role of power in our own lives.

As we complete Table 4.1 for ourselves, it might become apparent to us that in a single setting, we both have power and are

Power dynamics in my life	Resources	People
I have power over . . .		
. . . has power over me.		

TABLE 4.1

---

[45] Paolo Freire, *Pedagogy of the Oppressed* (New York: Continuum Publishing, 1997), 26.

subject to power. The cycle of oppressor and oppressed is a tight loop, not a grand narrative. We might also begin to feel sad. We want to be liberators and we want to liberate, but when that which really needs to change is something controlled by another who has power over us, our options are limited. My own experiences of burnout (see chapter 3) all share a common theme: I was being asked to do something I did not have the power to do, or I was imposing that unrealistic expectation on myself. That which really needed to happen in order for me to succeed was not within my purview to change. And yet I took it on nonetheless, like a woman standing between two mountains and being told to bring them a bit closer together. Sometimes the expectation was imposed upon me; when we are not the one with power, we do not always choose our mountains to move.

The appropriate change leadership stance to take in the midst of complex and competing power dynamics is walking a "critical path" between top-down and grassroots energies. That concept, weaving together power-with and empowering others, will become the theme of the later part of the chapter.

First, we take a close look at that which does not wish for a close look: how does power work? At its worst, how does it conceal itself in order to preserve itself? At its best, how do we use the power that we have to foster liberation in ourselves and others, so that all might find a deeper sense of connection with their communities and the world? The chapter will begin with an exploration of liberation theology and some ways in which liberationist ideas make a difference in communities today. Then we will consider concrete leadership strategies of walking a critical path between using our power and connecting with the energy source that is grassroots power, connecting top-down with bottom-up and causing those two ways in which change happens to join forces with one another.

Education for Liberation

The grandparent of the school of thought now known as "education for liberation" was Paolo Freire, the initiator of a movement to foster consciousness among agrarian workers in Brazil through stoking their curiosity and empowering them to get their questions answered. Freire's seminal book, *The Pedagogy of the Oppressed*, reflects the ideals of liberation theology, which understands Christ's teachings and resurrection most fully in Christ's upending of oppressive power structures. Famously, Freire scorned what he calls a "banking" style of teaching, where learners are treated like empty accounts waiting for deposits.[46] He emphasized the importance of humanizing those who are economically and politically disadvantaged rather than thinking of or treating them like objects. He encouraged creative and collaborative problem-solving; in his Brazilian context, economic development often meant outsiders with access to resources entered underprivileged communities and "instructed" those who knew the land best. The engine powering Freire's theory of change was conscientization, the active promotion of a co-learning mentality to foster partnership.

Freire wrote that liberationist education begins with a concrete problem that a multidisciplinary team can take on together, bringing together indigenous knowledge as well as intellectual expertise. He pointed out the tactics that oppressors use to hold onto power, such as dividing indigenous communities from one another and keeping them at odds with each other to prevent their developing consciousness of their oppression. He named the tactics of the powerful in ways that called out these nefarious and self-serving strategies in a time when, as now, power sustained itself by hiding in plain sight.

---

46 Ibid., 54.

All Need Liberation

These arguments for education for liberation might be unsurprising, even truistic. Less obvious is Freire's understanding of the need for liberation not just of the oppressed, but the oppressors.[47] If oppression is indeed cyclical and dialectical, as described previously, then we can expect that failing to break the cycle simply turns the oppressed into oppressors themselves. When an oppressor understands a person who works for her or him to be a "being for others"[48]—namely, a being for the oppressor's use and abuse—the oppressor plays a role in a sick system that twisted the idea of discipleship into a dehumanizing codependence. Those who oppress therefore must learn that they are playing a part in a cultural drama; what they are acting out is not freedom and is not real. "Those who authentically commit themselves to the people must reexamine themselves constantly."[49] The oppressors must become liberated because they have served as "host" to an oppressive power, having come to believe themselves to be human and others to be somehow less-than.[50] Until dialogue ensues, and understanding of each other's humanness flows from mutual recognition of humanity, no one is free.

How do leaders even enter into thinking about their roles as oppressors, let alone foster discussion on liberation? A good first step might be to consider, alone or with a group, the ways in which people can be different from each other. In classroom discussion, I often ask students, "In what ways are we all different from each other?" and then I write the words shared on the board. They usually include: age, race, gender, gender identity, ability, first language, country of origin, faith tradition, intelligence.

---

[47] Ibid., 26.

[48] Ibid., 30.

[49] Ibid., 42.

[50] Ibid., 30.

The list typically draws out more than twenty ways in which people are different from each other, and, in recent years, that number has increased as people have become more aware of unhelpful binaries around gender, race, and sexuality. I then ask the group to consider how the differences they name suggest power hierarchies, which move in many more directions than "up" and "down." The intersectionality of identities and power hierarchies is one way in which we can consider how each of us has power and yet is subject to power at the same time.

I use the example of myself to describe intersectionality: I am a white, cisgender woman (cisgender meaning that I not only identify as, but appear by stereotypical standards to be, a woman). I am straight, married, and a parent, which gives me certain credibility for the fact that I live out certain practices that make some more comfortable with me than they might be if I were lesbian, gender-nonconforming, or single. I am an adoptive parent of one child, so those with more than one birth child might consider me lesser, but those who are childless might be those over whom I have power for having done something "normal," "expected," and "celebrated" for a woman. I work outside the home in a gender-inclusive but male-dominated setting. With some this makes me more respectable; with others, I am subject to groundless assumptions as to where my priorities lay. Like most women, I can enumerate from memory dozens of experiences where my intersectional location has caused me confusion and, occasionally, harm. I have a sense of where I need to be liberated: from judgment regarding my beauty or lack thereof, my personality (to the minds of some overpowering when coming from a woman), from the projections of others regarding my marriage and parenting priorities.

But where do others need to be liberated from me? Serving as I did for many years at a small seminary, where the administrative staff had to carry out all the functions one would associate with a graduate school, I have supervised many people and made my share of mistakes. I have had to lay people off, fire people for cause, and eliminate positions that still had people in them. As an educator, I have graded students. As a dean, I have disciplined, suspended, and expelled students, placing a higher premium on community standards than individual human flourishing. Does this make me a bad person? Maybe some think so, and sometimes I feel like one. But more notably for the sake of this chapter, these dynamics are part of being a leader, where we have power over others, and others have power over us, all at the same time.

Robert Kegan, whose ideas about adult development appear in chapter 2, writes that we are *subject* to assumptions that are so embedded in us as to have been written like code into our cognitive functioning. The engine that powers our maturation is the movement of those subjective assumptions to an *objective* position, where once-tacit understandings become recognizable to us as the assumptions they are. We gain agency over them when we have a chance to examine and even revisit what we once took for granted.[51]

Like Kegan, Freire uses the concepts of "subject" and "object" to describe the way we make sense of the world around us. Freire uses the terms "subject" and "object" differently, but his ideas about human development are similar to Kegan's. He writes that we are subject to the power of those who control our access to the resources we need to live and flourish. When we have power over others, we consider them to be objects under our influence. When we become liberated, we realize that we are all subjects and we are all objects, just in different parts of our lives. Conscientization is the way in which we become aware of our subjectivity: we are not supporting characters in a play about those with power. We have our own narratives and are not just recipients of the power

51 Robert Kegan, *The Evolving Self: Problem and Process in Human Development* (Cambridge, MA: Harvard University Press, 1982).

of others. For the oppressed workers with whom Freire worked, he took their knowledge seriously. He entered dialogue with them and encouraged them to ask questions and seek answers to those questions. As they became conscious of what they knew and emboldened to ask questions, they began to create new knowledge—praxis—about how to live their own lives, not just strive after the life of others.

Those who are the recipients of power—Freire's oppressed—find agency and, when they realize they can, they seek control over the resources that make living possible. The process looks different for the one who has power over others. Those who have power might first become conscientized when they realize that exerting power over others has become ineffective. The road to liberation might begin with an internal sense of alienation or isolation, made manifest in an aching sense of meaninglessness. When it comes to intentional liberation, those with power enter in through dialogue.

Dialogical Leadership

In the television show "Undercover Boss,"[52] an executive puts on a disguise and a false identity as a low-ranking worker in the company she operates, owns, or both. The executive is made to look the fool when attempting to do the work that she once thought looked so easy. She forms relationships with those who train her and supervise her. Some are nice, and some are mean, and the viewer sees the true colors of the obsequious workers who fawn over executives but are then unkind to line workers. At the end of the show, the executive reveals her identity and confronts those who were unkind (which makes for good reality television), and rewards those who were supportive by providing promotions and bonuses. Without exception, the executive weeps when interviewed about what it was like to connect deeply with workers.

---

52 "Undercover Boss," CBS television series, Studio Lambert, 2010.

The ethical flaws of this show and the premise behind it leap to the eye. If the executive is truly transformed, why does she not ask why she makes a thousand times more money than the line workers? Individual promotions and small bonuses will have no effect on the system that, through structural injustice, placed the executive and those who work for the company in separate worlds. Bridging the gap is considered so outlandish as to be entertaining on reality TV, and yet the executive has experienced that bridge. She enters dialogue where there was once alienation and separateness.

Dialogue in itself is worthy and, to my mind, pleasing to God. Meaningful connection is a catalyst for change. Moments of recognition, where we see that categories divide us but relationships can still connect us, are intensely moving. Categories like boss and worker, teacher and student, and pastor and parishioner order the way we live together in community; they are not meaningless distinctions. But they are not unbreachable fortresses either. Dialogue leads to a dialectical and transformative connection that is the beginning of so many of life's true wonders: creativity, affection, freedom.

Therefore, a leader who wishes to bring about change begins with dialogue, and liberation of both the oppressor and the oppressed becomes possible. That liberation unleashes energies that power an organization to move in a life-giving direction. Practically speaking, dialogue helps a leader to know where the grassroots energy is located and how it might move the organization. Those who study change from a business perspective have long understood that tracking grassroots energy is essential to change leadership. In their article on how and why change programs do not work, business scholars Eisenstat, Spector, and Beer write that the mistake executives make when seeking to engineer a change in an organization is that they forget where change really comes from.[53]

---

53 Russel Eisenstat, Bert Spector, and Michael Beer, "Why Change Programs Don't Produce Change," *Harvard Business Review*, no. 11 (1990).

Leaders must track and follow the energy of the community and harness grassroots power. The authors suggest that change begins with shared problem diagnosis, so that all—both with power and subject to it—own that change is needed. They define the role of leaders as coordination, mobilizing commitment, and promoting cohesion. In this role, leaders spur and institutionalize revitalization; they do not create it.

Although Eisenstat, Spector, and Beer come from an explicitly capitalistic point of view as professors from a world-renowned business school, their ideas resonate with Freire's. The notion that the key to change is harnessing the power that comes from those who are led, and mobilizing it toward a shared goal, is a common denominator in these writings from divergent sources. Perhaps even more resonant is the work of Agusto Boal, pioneer of the movement known now as Theater of the Oppressed.[54] Like Freire, Boal's work took place in Brazil in the 1960s and 1970s, a time when that country was just beginning to exhibit the extremes of opulence and poverty that are now even more prevalent. Boal's social justice work began as theater for those in extreme poverty, where actors incited peasants to stand up to their oppressors. Over time, he and his theater troupe came to understand that promoting justice to others, for others, was not sufficient if the ultimate goal is liberation.

Boal and his theater troupe evolved from presenting plays that fostered consciousness of oppression to improvising plays using suggestions from their audiences on the problems in their communities. Even this transformation did not go far enough, for it was the actors who were suggesting resolution to the problems of those in poverty, as though those in poverty had no capacity for resolving their own problems. Today, hundreds have learned how to use the improvisational methodology developed by Boal where those in the

---

54 Agusto Boal, *The Rainbow of Desire: The Boal Method of Theatre and Therapy*, trans. Adrian Jackson (London and New York: Routledge), 1995.

audience both present and solve their problems. The technique involves audience members embodying their suffering, using imagination and metaphor, and then physically enacting what resolution might look like, also metaphorically. The expression "creative problem-solving" takes on a literary structure in Theater of the Oppressed.

Boal writes that the experience of oppression is not transferable,[55] meaning that no one can adequately imagine what it is like to be another person, especially a person who is suffering. And yet imagination is essential to leadership and change for communities. Change leadership involves imagining a new reality and then taking actions that make that imagined vision real. Yet leaders who seek to imagine *for* the community over whom they have power continue the cycle of oppression. Leaders who imagine *with* the community are the only leaders capable of bringing about change.

Coordinating Energies

I have used expressions like "top-down" and "grassroots" forms of power with little explanation of what those forms of power mean. Top-down can best be understood as power that is institutionalized, formal, structured, and codified. We listen to an elected leader because that leader has been authorized to hold their position. Those with authorization enact policies that might have originated in the community, but then the community delegated responsibility for enforcement to the leader. For instance, I as dean of a faculty was authorized to hold the faculty accountable to policies that the faculty itself had created and affirmed. When the faculty pushed back against that accountability, it was mine to ask the question as to whether the policies needed to be revisited. Those with top-down power do not have complete control over communities. Power is impure, and top-down merely notes where the power comes from, not its ultimate effectiveness.

---

[55] Ibid., 3.

Grassroots power is aptly named. Grass is organic and often indigenous to the soil in which it grows, and grassroots power is not created by institutions, but rather it grows up out of communities. Grass grows from the earth upward, and unlike power from institutions are top-down, grassroots power is earthy and grows from the bottom up. Under the earth, the roots of grass are small and fragile; they are also interconnected. Grassroots movements are easily torn up but also highly networked.

The energies of power could also be likened to stalactites and stalagmites, the rock formations we find inside caves. Stalactites come down from the upper reaches of the cave, and the stalagmites grow up from the ground. Both result from mineral deposits, and they often appear to be reaching down and up toward one another, even though their patterns do not insist on eventual connection with each other. I like to think of stalactites and stalagmites as images for the top-down power that comes from institutions and the bottom-up power that emerges from communities. Both are power, which means either can be used toward the good or the ill. Both are made up of the same component parts but behave differently due to bigger forces. The image of these rock formations provides a visual depiction of the most effective form of change leadership.

In Figure 4.1, this graphic depiction of change leadership in the midst of power dynamics, the stalactites represent top-down, or institutionalized power. Top-down power takes the form of agreed-upon and articulated policies that designate some as having authority. Elected or appointed leaders, empowered representatives, and even institutions themselves hold this kind of power. It is neither bad nor good inherently, although one could easily argue that the one in possession of such power is more vulnerable to corruption because of top-down power's seductive potential to bring about change irrespective of the will of the community. The advantage of holding top-down power is that those who have it can effect change more easily than the one who must build a coalition from the ground up. The disadvantage is the view: those whose power comes from the top have to work hard to see those who are led. Perhaps because they have little incentive to do so, those with power can be oblivious to the needs and capacities of those over whom they have power.

The stalagmites in this diagram represent those with grass-roots, bottom-up power. The power that grows up from the ground might take longer to accrue. Stalagmites might be shorter due to the force of gravity, but they are stronger for the same

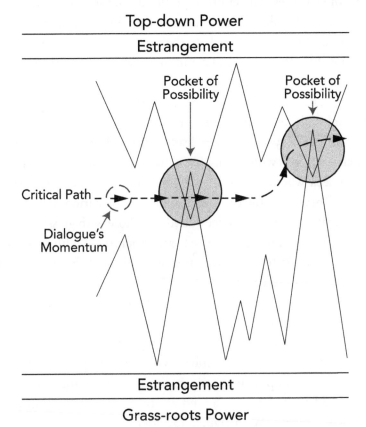

FIGURE 4.1

reason. As in a cave, the space between the stalagmites and the stalactites in this diagram is dark and void until light is cast onto it. This need for light represents how power dynamics function in invisibility and can only be appreciated and explored when illuminated. When illuminated, and the complexity of the interaction between top-down and bottom-up varieties of power are exposed, we see possibilities we might not have imagined. A leader cannot move two rock formations closer together without snapping off complex structures that have built themselves up and down over years or centuries. Any effort to physically connect the stalagmites or stalactites would either be futile or would result in destruction. That said, noticing and tracking their patterns is both worthwhile and possible. The leader and community who can recognize power structures are most likely to use power for the purpose of change, rather than finding change stymied constantly as power dynamics exert invisible and baffling influence.

The pathway that carries leaders through the empty space, which is charged with possibility, is dialogue. Those with top-down power seek where energy is emerging from those with grassroots power. They do so by learning, listening, and sharing in a process of generating new knowledge and ideas. Those with grassroots and those with top-down power need each other: those with grassroots power need institutional structural strength, and those with top-down power need energy.

The places where the stalagmites and the stalactites find themselves in close proximity to one another are what I call pockets of possibility. Just yesterday, I found myself in conversation with a leader from my denomination's national setting who wants to form a partnership with a seminary focused on environmental justice. I had invited him to attend a forum at our school on environmental justice. We imagined together what it would be like to provide institutional support to student activism around creation justice. What if we were to create a funded position for one of the student activists to offer community organizing for ecology ministries? What if we were to create an online repository of resources to capture and disseminate accumulated wisdom of our faith tradition on environmental activism? What if? What if? What if?

A visual depiction of our conversation—which we can see in Figure 4.1—might have looked like us imagining what we, holding authorized positions in strong institutions, could do to connect with the energy that is already coming up from the ground in our community. As Eisenstat, Spector, and Beer tell us, the leader's job is to plug grassroots energies into the machinery of change leadership. The alternative to reaching out through dialogue is an unsatisfactory estranged baseline for both those with top-down and with grassroots power. Finding shared motivation through identifying pockets of possibility for collaboration is a better way to participate in the institutions that form our society than isolation that prevents transformation.

Consider this illustration: I have a pastor colleague who likes to joke that he is the laziest minister in the world. Every time someone comes to him with an idea for him, he says, "That sounds great! Go for it!" and although he offers to help, he does not implement the ideas of others. He intuitively realizes that the best thing he can do is empower his congregation where their energy lies. He never originates ideas, but he has a knack for reading whether enough energy exists that he can help to mobilize. He also connects those with ideas to resources, including other people with similar ideas and energies. In the end, his approach is not lazy at all, but rather it is ecological in that it uses energy efficiently.

Dismantling Oppressive Structures

You might be uncomfortable with the notion of working within power structures, especially those that are unjust. Certainly, this diagram could suggest that those with top-down power press down, manipulating those without it. Power is not inherently corrupt, but it corrupts. If the mission of an organization is to steal from the poor and further enrich the rich, then this analysis of power dynamics can sicken one who cares about social justice. Consider cigarette marketing campaigns in the 1980s that targeted children and teens, for example, when corporations entered a dialogue of sorts with consumers and figured out what would get their attention: a cartoon of a camel.

What is the difference between top-down and grassroots partnership that leads to manipulation versus liberation? The catalytic power of mutual dialogue. Dialogue promotes shared understanding for all stakeholders, so that everyone changes in some way. Renowned community organizer Saul Alinsky, influenced by the key precepts of liberation theology, built his movement on the following principles: (1) those with control over resources do not listen, (2) the oppressed are different from each other, and (3) the oppressed do not believe they can effect change.[56] Like Boal, the foundation on which he built a methodology for partnering with the oppressed took into consideration that oppressors not only control resources. They also control narratives that whole communities use to make sense of their life situations.[57] Part of that narrative reads, "You do not know what's best for you," and, "You cannot change your situation."

Those with control over resources do not listen. We have all had the experience where we have felt like one who has power over us does not—cannot—listen to us. Because people with power have control over resources and narrative, they do not have to listen. Nothing bad comes to them immediately for not listening, until, of course, they find their influence waning. Because the very nature of power causes a certain deafness to set in, leaders who want to bring about change must train themselves to listen.

---

[56] Gregory Galluzzo, "Faith-Based Organizing—a Justice Ministry: A Strategy for Ministry," *International Journal of Public Theology* 3 (2009), 109.

[57] Boal, *The Rainbow of Desire*, 8.

One way in which leaders do this is through building structures of evaluative practice. They collaborate with those they lead on setting goals, and then they use surveys, focus groups, and interview strategies to gather data on how they are meeting those goals. Amidst power differentials, casual dialogue is rare and often impersonal, and evaluation provides necessary structure. And these practices can be adapted, humanized. For instance, a minister who decides to meet with every family in the congregation over the course of the year is, in a way, conducting interviews. The one who writes an email that includes a request for feedback is conducting a survey. The one who includes reflective discussion on a meeting agenda is conducting a focus group.

Another way in which leaders can overcome their disinclination toward listening is to take extremely good care of themselves. Hearkening back to chapter 3, leaders who are clear in their self-differentiation are better listeners. They know that they are separate from those they lead, yet together with their community. They are part of the community but also whole. Hearing something they might not want to hear is thus less threatening to their identities. For that reason, they are better able to listen because they do not assume they know what they are about to hear. Leaders who take good care of their relationships, bodies, and inner lives are less likely to forget who they are and therefore who they are not.

The oppressed are different from each other. The goals that exist within a community might vary, and, in that variation, the community's power and influence can become diluted. Alinsky worked in community organizing to help those who were in most ways different to come together around a common goal. One of the most common and effective strategies of the oppressor is to divide and conquer. Even from a disconnected distance, oppressors know that those over whom they exert power have internal distinctions, one from the other. Oppressors work to highlight those differences, lest those whom they oppress find one another, share their stories, and realize that they have the capacity to make a difference. They encourage those they oppress to fear each other, avoid each other, and see one another as "other."

In his seminal and disturbing book *Evicted*,[58] Matthew Desmond describes dozens of policies that undermine the attempts of the poor in urban America to find stable housing. One policy that concretely illustrates a divide-and-conquer oppressive use of power makes it difficult for extended families who rely on public funding assistance to reside under one roof. Furthermore, landlords can easily reject rental applications or evict tenants whose children behave like . . . children. Liberative leaders foster togetherness through dialogue that fosters understanding. They help those they lead to put aside irrelevant differences that are not important in light of specific communal concerns, and they focus on a shared cause.

Imagine a situation where an executive director in a social justice organization senses a lack of energy in the board that might be resulting, in part, from a conflict over a budgetary issue. Helping the board to remember and articulate a common purpose is one way for the leader to remind the group that its budget dispute is not as important as the organization's mission, which is what brought them together in the first place. Imagine another situation, where the same executive director reads in the news about an oncoming threat from a governmental policy change. Joining together with other organizations on addressing this common cause, no matter how different those other organizations might be, is the best way to prepare to confront those who have more power. Oppressors seek to alienate communities from one another, and liberative leaders help members of communities find common ground.

---

58 Matthew Desmond, *Evicted: Poverty and Profit in the American City* (Milan: Daily Books, 2017).

Habits and Disciplines of Liberative Leaders

Is power a force within people, which they can either use or abuse depending on their ethical fiber, faith, and education? Is power a force unto itself that uses individuals as its carrier, seeking out a will all its own? The latter possibility becomes more plausible when we consider all that power will do to preserve itself. Like homeostasis, described in chapter 3, power will seek to retain the status quo and has self-preservation properties more like a virus than an independent organism. When it is threatened, it mutates. When it finds a compatible host, it takes over, and frequently the host is caused to suffer.

Recall the example from the introduction I used of Kyle, a young professional associated with an organization I support who came to me for some free leadership coaching. Kyle was young, bright, optimistic, and capable. Many in the church wondered how Kyle had advanced so quickly, so young. He had set the appointment under the guise of seeking professional advice. In reality, Kyle wanted to talk with me about his plans to confront an unhealthy dynamic in the organization he served, where the second-in-command was dysfunctional and undermining the organization's effectiveness. I listened actively, asking questions and affirming that the dynamics Kyle was seeing were indeed worrisome. Because he was right, and because he was smart, Kyle believed that he had all he needed to go to the organization's executive to start the process of excising the unhealthy staff person from the organization. I told him he was wrong.

Kyle had underestimated the way in which power was keeping the dysfunction in place, and what kind of power would be necessary to shake the equilibrium. Whatever power that was, it was not in his hands. The nonfunctioning staff person was there for a reason, had stuck for a reason, and how and why Kyle had accumulated so much power was the only really surprising result.

I repeated to Kyle words my own mentor had once said to me in a similar situation: this is going to come unglued, but not because of you. Kyle did not agree with me. He thought that since he had the institution's best interest on his side, and since he was right, he could—had to—go directly to the executive and insist the person not functioning well needed to go. Within six weeks of his meeting with me, Kyle was no longer on staff.

If power is indeed so stubborn, elusive, as difficult to handle as uranium, and just as capable of creating energy, how can leaders even begin to think about using and managing it? First, leaders must acknowledge that they have power. If they control some resources, or if they have opportunities to tell stories that shape reality, they have power. Second, they must commit to sharing that power. The following practices, when attended to regularly and with self-discipline, help leaders to use the power they have toward liberative ends.

- Track grassroots energy and attend to areas where the community is inspired.
- Consider the vulnerable at every turn.
- Empower to lead those who would otherwise be subject to the action of leaders.
- Use the arts, spirituality, and relationship-building to disrupt the entrenched flow of power.
- Embrace dialogue; assume nothing.
- Beware the quick fix and allow dialogue to do its slow but lasting work.
- Focus on attending to disconnects between espoused and operational values in the organization and in ourselves.

One surefire way *not* to lead liberatively is to pretend that power does not exist. Those who mistake denying power's reality for misuse of power are likely to make clueless assumptions, treat individuals like masses, and fail to listen. Those who have power must train their minds to think first about those over whom they have power, the ones who are both vulnerable and who could help a change to be truly transformational. When initiating a renovation project, we ask, "Who might not be able to access it in its new design?" When we catch wind of a scandal involving a teacher we supervise, we ask, "Who might have been subject to that teacher's power, and therefore a potential victim, and what might that victim need?" Leaders who do not discipline their minds to consider the vulnerable will revert to habits of self-preservation, power preservation, and institutional preservation. This does not make those with power bad people; it makes them people. For heaven's sake, we must be better.

Power in Context, among Dynamics

There are choices that leaders must make in real time if they embrace liberation: dialogue (not speaking for others or making assumptions), relationships (not just transactions, and among equals in the eyes of God), and building community (rather than encampments in our comfort zones). Liberationist leaders walk what can sometimes be a poorly marked path between top-down and grassroots power, seeking pockets of possibility, propelled by dialogue.

We return now to the theoretical framework introduced in chapter 1 and the places where reason, emotion, and power are situated.

As described previously, the three dynamics of change are situated in locations meant to suggest that reason is closer to the leadership terrain—yet a narrower portion of the triangle—than are emotion and power. In other words, reasoning with a community about vision, necessary steps, and hoped-for outcomes is relatively straightforward, but it is also relatively superficial. Emotion takes place at a deeper and more foundational level. Power is deeper still, and more elusive to those seeking change from the leadership terrain. It is impervious to reason and emotion alike.

What we see in the structure of the theoretical framework is a cascade of underestimation, starting from the leadership terrain. Leaders tend to underestimate how much communicating they need to do, and how much planning is required to bring about change. They make the mistake of thinking that all they need to do is explain a change one time, and then the community will buy in. More commonly and dangerously, leaders make the mistake named by Friedman of placing unreasonable faith in people being reasonable.[59] Even the most arduously articulated plan is only as likely to be accepted as the emotional context will allow it to be.

We cannot underestimate the importance of teaching, communicating, and planning, yet we also must recognize that reason is not as powerful as emotion. Communities make collective decisions that seem irrational for the simple, tautological reason that the decisions do not emerge from reason. Rather they come out of a community's emotions, for good or for ill. An example is the choice I see in struggling theological schools to launch new programs whose educational model may be sound, but whose financial model holds no water. This is not a rational choice, but the emotion of hope in the new model overtakes mathematical reasoning. And sometimes it works.

More perilous still, and less avoidable, is the tendency we have to underestimate the trump card of power. Take a moment to consider how often you have worked hard to bring a change about, only to have a person with more money and more influence undo your efforts with a word or a glance. We can remember the frustration at the unfairness of such situations months or even years later. Can you remember a case where the reverse was true: you were the one with the power and influence scuttling the idea or project of another? Chances are you cannot, but the likelihood you have never undermined another person in your workplace, family, or

---

59 Friedman, *A Failure of Nerve.*

church is exceedingly low. You do not remember because you were the one with the power. Your power blinded you to the impact of your own actions; you were its host. Is power therefore evil? No, it is like physics: devoid of moral substance but rather a vessel for doing good or ill. But the work we do to become more aware of its nature and presence is worthwhile if we want to use power to the good. Consciousness of power dynamics helps us to take advantage of that which can be accomplished when different forms of power find a common cause.

Power can be perverse or inspiring depending on its use. The main caution levied in this chapter related to top-down power is a word to the wise that those with power are essentially blind and deaf to those over whom they have power. The scales can fall from the eyes of those who carry top-down power as they become enlightened as to how oppression works, just as those who have grassroots power can become conscientized to their collective potential. Power can erase the good work of educating and planning associated with reason, and it can topple what we thought were the healthiest boundaries in an emotional system. Accepting power's winner-takes-all nature, and approaching it with the creativity of an alchemist, is the leadership strategy most likely to effect change. That alchemy requires locating the connections between the goals of those with top-down and grassroots power and mixing together those two potent energies for leadership.

In this chapter, I have explored the nature of power in the midst of organizational change. I used the foundation of liberation theology to build an approach to leading in the midst of power, where potential lies in the space between grassroots energies and power lodged in formal, institutional entities. Dialogue, relationships, and community building are the activities that can take place within that space, with transformational change as the sought-after ends. The chapter closed with a reflection on how reason, emotion, and power are each in-turn underestimated as relates to their importance in ways that undermine leaders' effectiveness. In chapter 5 we move to the final section of the theoretical framework guiding this book: the leadership terrain itself, and how it cries out to leaders to discern God's will for our work and our world.

 ## Exercise: Case Study—The Call of Cruella

Monique's most formative experiences as a young person were participating in mission trips with her church. The first time she signed up for a trip, she was fourteen and in her first year of high school. Her main objectives were to get to fly in an airplane, go somewhere warm during the winter, get a tan, and maybe even become friends with the popular older girls on the trip. Her experience spending a week in an impoverished but utterly joyful neighborhood, playing with kids while the adults on the trip refurbished a school building, moved her in ways she never thought possible. She felt like she was closer to the young participants on the trip after just a few days than she was with anyone with whom she had gone to school her whole life. The adults on the trip marveled at how happy and outgoing Monique became on the trip, where they previously might have described her as shy and serious. Monique keeps a picture of herself on that first trip, playing helicopter—spinning around—with a five-year-old from the neighborhood where she served, on her desk. She looks at the picture every time she feels down, as it reminds her who she is and focuses her on her emerging sense of call.

Monique's parents were not part of that trip, or any of the four subsequent ones that functioned like a plumb line drawing her into adulthood. Her mother's chronic fatigue syndrome and her father's work schedule made such travel impossible. They never really understood why Monique wanted to go to work while on a school vacation, and they definitely did not understand the $1500 price tag on her plane ticket and travel costs. When she returned from trips, as they had no frame of reference for what Monique experienced, they asked few questions. By the third one, she was saving up all her babysitting money from the year to pay her own way, and Monique barely talked with her parents about the trip at all.

During and after the first trip, as Monique felt like the world was tilting on its axis, she spent more and more time with the church's youth minister, Heather. Heather was in seminary at the time, and she co-led the first two trips Monique experienced. After Heather graduated from seminary and moved on, the two stayed in touch. By her junior year in high school, Monique was taking on more and more of a leadership role on her church's trips, and Heather was a source of advice and a sounding board. In addition to the advice she received, Monique became a supporter and encourager to Heather, as Heather weathered a turbulent transition into ministry in a setting where her gifts were, to Monique's mind, not adequately appreciated. It seemed only logical to Monique that she would follow the same path as Heather and go straight from college to seminary, so she did, to the utter bafflement of her family.

When Monique entered divinity school, Heather was more settled into ministry in a far-away city. She hired Monique to come to that city and lead spring break trips in a church that had not experienced service trips before. Although doing so tore her away from her divinity school community during a busy time of year that always seemed to fall during midterms, and participation required taking time off from a supervised ministry setting where things never seemed to click, Monique led trips for three years running. In doing so, she and Heather together built a new tradition for the congregation that both transformed its youth program and gave Monique a clear sense of call: she would become a social justice educator, and travel seminars would be her specialty.

In the fall of Monique's final year in her MDiv program, Hurricane Cruella hit the city of Silver Bay, Florida. News reports of resorts and vacation homes washed away shocked viewers. Flooding had reached so far inland that jellyfish were found on sidewalks in neighborhoods miles from the shore. The recovery would take months, if not years, said reporters, and damage from Hurricane Cruella lay bare income disparities and systemic injustice in the region hit by the storm. Millionaires found contractors to rebuild their vacation homes, but the local schools remained closed for weeks due to damage and mold. Those living in mobile homes and shacks were unable to live in their residences and could not afford to leave. Monique became fixated on tracking storm damage to the point where her studies suffered. Her sense of connection to the suffering in Silver Bay tugged at her constantly.

Heather called Monique two months after the storm, when news stories had all but evaporated but relief efforts in Florida were barely making headway, to tell her about an amazing coincidence and opportunity. One of Heather's seminary classmates had started a nonprofit in Florida that hosted youth programs year-round. The nonprofit was located—you guessed it—in Silver Bay. Heather described Cliff as a dear friend who, after graduation, went to Florida to become an associate pastor. While serving there, he came up with the idea for a youth ministry program that would teach teens how to sail as a means of teaching them teamwork skills and respect for creation. "Soul Sailing" had to seriously rethink its mission after Hurricane Cruella. Half the sailing school's fleet was destroyed in the storm, and the rest needed expensive repairs. Parents were not excited about sending their kids to Silver Bay. Cliff had spun the organization off the church he had served, creating an independent nonprofit organization, and he needed to think fast to make sure Soul Sailing would—ironically—stay afloat.

Heather wanted Monique to take the church's youth group on its mission trip to Soul Sailing in Silver Bay during that spring break, and Monique was elated to do so. She had felt so drawn to the tragedy there, and the chance during her last months in divinity school to go with a group of adults and youth she had come to love seemed a fitting end to her studies. Heather surprised Monique with one thing more: "While you are there, Cliff wants to talk with you about what you are doing after graduation," said Heather. "He's looking to hire a travel seminar coordinator, and I've told him that you are the only person I could imagine recommending."

The feeling that all was falling into place perfectly gave Monique a deep sense of peace and trust in God's plan for her life. She connected with Cliff about the spring break trip she would lead, and because she knew what to do to plan a great trip, she instantly wowed Cliff with her confidence and skill. When the group arrived in Silver Bay, they drove through destruction unlike anything Monique had ever seen. She, the youth and adults from the trip, and the hired bus driver all had tears streaming down their faces by the time they reached the headquarters of Soul Surfer. When they got there, Cliff ran out to meet them. The group was tired and dirty after the eighteen-hour trip one day, sleeping on a church floor, and then the six hours driving that morning, but Cliff put them to work right away anyway learning the basics of sailing small skiffs. Monique had thought for sure that they would be helping Cliff with repairs, and then enabling youth in the area to take advantage of time at sea to get away from their troubles and find empowerment and encouragement. She quickly realized, however, that Cliff wanted the group to have a fun time, post pictures online highlighting Soul Surfing at its best, and help him to market his program to a skittish public.

Cliff and Heather had been seminary classmates, and evidently had even dated briefly (Heather broke his heart, Cliff was quick to volunteer to this group of Heather's parishioners). He saw his relationship with Monique as an extension of Heather's relationship with Monique, but the two had never met before this trip. Over the course of the week, Monique found herself constantly surprised by choices Cliff was making. Cliff had no instincts for how people would want to spend their time. He said that he wanted to become part of the relief effort in Silver Bay but, even having lived there for years, he had no relationships in the community. The group had come to work, and he tried to convince them that what they really needed to do was learn how to sail. Monique could sense their restlessness.

Three days in, Monique asked Cliff if they could talk about how the schedule would work for the remainder of the week. In their conversation, Monique worried she was stepping far out of bounds, giving Cliff direct feedback on how things were going, and what she felt needed to change: the group needs to get into the community, they need to contribute to relief efforts, no more sailing school. Instead of taking offense, Cliff swept Monique up into a hug and spun her around . . . like a helicopter. "This is why I need you to come and build this ministry with me!" he exclaimed. "You have the knowledge, gifts, and skill I need. Please come work with me after graduation: I'm begging you."

For discussion:

1. How do power dynamics influence the various stakeholders in this case?
2. How might a liberationist approach to change leadership inform the work of Soul Sailing?
3. How does Monique's advice to Cliff about reorganizing the trip reflect a liberationist perspective?
4. Make Monique a list of pros and cons for taking this job opportunity, using reason, emotion, and power as criteria.

5. If you were to write an epilogue to this case study based on what you think would be a good outcome for all, what would it say happened next?

 Exercise: Case Study—Chaplain Martha

Martha has served St. John's Academy as chaplain for seven years. She coordinates a weekly chapel service and teaches a required course on moral reasoning to sophomores. Everything she has ever known about moral reasoning she had to learn in order to teach her sophomore course. Her undergraduate major in English prepared her to look for moral questions and how literary characters resolved them. During her divinity school years, she took several electives in social justice and liberation theology, which persuaded St. John's to see her as qualified to teach ethics. She did not mention during her interviews that she had taken only one ethics course in divinity school and had not dedicated much attention to it. It will take a crisis at St. John's to question how her role as an instructor in moral reasoning fit into her role outside the classroom.

Martha lives on campus in a dormitory that houses thirteen sophomore and junior girls, plus two seniors who have sought-after leadership roles as prefects. Martha was in a long-distance intimate-partner relationship when she came to St. John's, but in her first year she found herself in a confusingly intense friendship with another teacher—Max—that had her significant other jealous from afar and eventually bitter. Martha did serious soul-searching as to what her deep sense of connection with Max meant, and she came to understand it indicated a missing connection with her intimate partner. After trying to make things work in her long-distance relationship, with weekend visits and Skype conversations that began to feel like work, Martha eventually decided that, even though she and Max were not heading for romance (he was in a long-distance relationship too), she needed to break things off.

Max married his long-distance love, and Martha was considering reentering the dating fray when crisis ensued.

Martha saw Max departing her dormitory at 11:45 PM on a Tuesday. She was in her pajamas and had decided to take out some foul-smelling trash she worried might ripen overnight when she saw him leaving from a back stairway exit. "Max!" she said, and Max immediately turned up his collar and began to walk quickly away. "Max!" she said again, and he made a dramatic about-face, making direct and yet sheepish eye contact. "What are you doing here?" asked Martha.

"Alyssa . . . needed some extra help on a calculus problem, and I must have lost track of time," said Max. Alyssa was one of the prefects in Martha's dorm. A beautiful, promising student-athlete, Alyssa was unusually mature and at times aloof. Unlike previous prefects, she had not once confided in Martha any of her vulnerabilities or worries about the future. In fact, she had never talked with Martha about anything other than issues in the dorm.

"Max, this is so not-cool," said Martha. "It's lights-out, and . . . and . . . well, this just looks bad."

"And that's why you're not going to mention it, Martha," said Max, with a penetrating look. "It does look bad. It makes both of us look bad." For a second, Martha thought Max was referring to himself and Alyssa. But immediately, Martha realized he was referring to himself, and to her, Martha. Martha reeled back in shock. Was Max threatening her? Was he suggesting it was Martha who had done something wrong? Was he basically admitting that what he was doing with Alyssa was worthy of the suspicion his late-night departure elicited? "Tomorrow, we're talking about this, Max," said Martha. "Tomorrow it is, Chaplain Martha," he replied and hastily made his way down the driveway to his own residence.

Martha did not sleep a wink that night. Early in the morning, rather than seeking out Max, she knocked on the door of her head of school, Andrew. As the chaplain and a teacher of moral reasoning, she was more than a little embarrassed to be found on the front step of the head's residence unshowered and in sweatpants, and even more embarrassed when she burst into tears as soon as he opened the door. "So what you're saying is that we have a problem," said Andrew, causing Martha to interrupt her tears with a bout of laughter. Martha told Andrew everything: about the incident the night before, Max's suspicious and intimidating reaction to her questions, and about Max's and her previous edge-skirting relationship. The two constructed a plan where Andrew would initiate an investigation of the incident, which would include but not be managed by Martha. She left Andrew's home relieved, but realizing her life was about to get a lot harder before it would be easy again.

Before the end of the week, a moving truck was in front of Max's house on-campus. He was summarily dismissed after Alyssa admitted that she and her math teacher had been engaged in a sexual relationship for the better part of a year. Max's spouse, who had been well-liked by the boys in Max's dorm and by teachers, was the first to point to Martha as a culpable party. She posted a photo of Martha and Max from their first year teaching together with the hashtag, #hellhathnofury. Martha heard about the tweet and went straight to Andrew again. Andrew admitted that Max had, when confronted, suggested Martha reported his late-night dormitory departure out of jealous vindictiveness. Martha was floored not just at the frivolous, petty accusation, but by how wrong she had been about Max, whom she had so recently considered a friend.

In the midst of grief, shame, and fear for her own reputation, Martha has a chaplain's office to run, and she has a moral reasoning class to teach. Imagine she has come to you seeking specific help in making sense of this crisis in light of her role. She has a therapist helping her handle her emotions, and a career coach helping her on the power dynamics she is encountering. But she wants you—a peer with a similar position in another school—to lend your clear head to discernment about her professional responsibilities.

1. What are the power dynamics at work in this situation? Who has power over whom, and where has power caused tensions to flare?
2. Help Martha by mapping out a plan for how she will handle this issue as a professional.
3. How might Martha incorporate cases like these into her teaching on moral reasoning?

Gifts for Change Leadership

An effective leader amidst change is considerate and justice-minded. Does "considerate" strike you as a weak word when we think of liberation from oppression? That said, the first casualty of our failure to consider others is justice. When we regard other people as people, rather than objects or means to an end, a lot of other dimensions of life in community start going right. When we forget the humanity of others, everything starts going wrong. Justice-mindedness requires of us attention to power dynamics and acknowledgement of their shaping effects. With those over whom we have power, we must remember to be fair. With those who have power over us, we must remember to be collaborative, seeking out common interests and "partnering up" in ways that make our communities better.

We hone skills for being considerate using the previous two sets of practices. One who is organized and communicative has attentional capacity for noticing the vulnerable and making plans so that change does not disadvantage them. The leader who is communicative remembers that those who have less power need more communication, not less, about the way change might affect them. A grounded person is able to sense the wholeness of others.

A differentiated person does not get swept up in the drama of change to the point where human costs are forgotten. Practices of wellness that promote groundedness also foster compassion.

Undergirding each of these leadership gifts is the practice of paying attention. In a distracted age, leaders who are under pressure often lose track of what is happening around them. Noticing gives way to caring. Caring gives way to loving. Loving is at the heart of life-giving change. When we love our communities, we want what is best for them. We might have heard it said, "God loves us just as we are, and too much to allow us to stay as we are." May we love those we serve in ways that imitate this godly love, balancing our delight in that which is, with our determination to strive toward what can be.

.•5

Discernment on the Leadership Terrain

Discerning Needs and Choosing Strategies

The dynamics at work in change—reason, emotion, and power—each have correlative leadership practices that we blend, mix, and match to the situations in which we find ourselves. In this final chapter, we consider how we know when to choose which leadership practice. We first examine that question in terms of discernment: the communal practice of reading a situation and deciding how to live into it. We then consider the shape of the leadership terrain and what it takes strategically to blend approaches in real time, making choices about how to proceed and what practices to employ.

As the framework suggests, the leadership terrain itself is mysterious to us. It is space between us, in all our incarnate humanity, and a leadership situation similarly concrete. In that nebulous, in-between space, we have infinite choices and possibilities to consider, any of which could make that situation better or worse. No easy answers float through the leadership terrain, but the good news is that no one approach is the only "right" one.

Communal Discernment Practices

How do we, as leaders, know what change is the right change to make? Once we know, how do we read dynamics and choose leadership strategies? Many rely on their guts in reading options and choosing approaches. When working with a group, the gut of the individual is a help, but it is not enough to build a communal sense of direction.

Discernment is the connective tissue between leadership and the will of God. Discernment and leadership are not interchangeable terms, although they inform one another and rely on one another. Leadership without discernment is mere management, or maintenance. Discernment without leadership is a séance. Discernment involves disciplined, intentional, and deliberative exploration of God's intention for a person or community. Communal discernment requires a plan.

Three different practices of communal discernment originate from different schools of thought: career psychology, the ethics of authenticity, and theology. All three focus on discernment of vocation, rooted in the Latin "vocare" or "to call." For the purpose of change theory, we focus on communal practices of vocational discernment rather than personal practices, although each comes from theory intended for individuals.

Trait-factor congruence. First, from the field of career psychology, we borrow the term, "trait-factor." A trait refers to a characteristic of a person that defines who they are. A factor is a characteristic of a profession, task, or role. In individual career discernment, a person might have the trait "enjoys being with people." A career might have a factor "includes working with people." The match between the trait and the factor indicate a strong likelihood of happiness and success with that particular career match. When we expand trait-factor thinking to an organization or group, we are reminded that no group can be all things to all people. We are also reminded that the terrain on which organizations function has particularities we must take into account.

Trait-factor matches result in, to use a term borrowed by career psychology from geometry: "congruence." Just as two congruent shapes mirror each other, a trait-factor match results in a happy symmetry whose likelihood of success is high. As a matter of habit, many of us already think in terms of congruence. We say of a young couple, "They seem well-suited to one another." We explain an un-happy employee who is obviously gifted but not able to find success or satisfaction in a particular role as "a bad fit." In an increasingly diverse culture, we must become more disciplined than ever about surfacing the assumptions that lie, and do not lie, beneath our in-stinctive understandings of what does and does not fit. A couple that makes for a good fit, for example, likes and gets along with each other; their "fit" is not determined by their ethnicity. Likewise an employee is a good match, not because he is the office socialite, but because he likes the job, brings needed skills, and is effective. We must check our tendencies to bring in irrelevant and unjust criteria when analyzing trait-factor congruence.

For the purpose of communal discernment to ascertain con-gruence, we ask questions like these: What is the nature of this community? What are its contours and most notable attributes? We follow on with questions about the nature of our context. What are the needs of this community? What are its demograph-ics, and what do we know about the constitutive groups within it? Organizations have traits. Communities have factors. A disci-plined approach to finding matches between them is the essence of a theory of change (see chapter 1).

Consider this example: I am currently working to develop a faith-tradition–specific educational model within an ecumenical divinity school's general educational program. In this particular discernment, I am constantly naming what constitutes the faith traditions in question, while also naming the particular contours of the divinity school. I must define educational practices that both reflect the faith tradition *and* make sense in the context. I try not to waste energy bemoaning either the expectations of the faith traditions I serve, nor the limitations of the context. Both offer far more exciting opportunities than onerous restrictions, so I give my energy to where I find a good fit. If we find matches between what the tradition needs and what the divinity school can accommodate, our lives will be easier and success more likely, just like any case where traits and factors coexist (namely, in every relationship under the sun).

Trait-factor analysis for communal discernment has some distinct limitations. First, it assumes a great deal of knowledge about oneself or one's organization. Most of us know something about our strengths and weaknesses, but others of them are mysteries to us. Similarly, members of a community might think their organization has certain strengths and weaknesses; put simply, they can be wrong. Consider the church that understands itself to be welcoming and hospitable, but where visitors never return, having felt like guests at a stranger's family reunion. Testing and receiving feedback on traits and factors are essential due to the limitations of human perceptivity and the complexity of the coexistence of differing views.

Just like a young person starting out in the working world, sometimes we learn who we are and how our nature matches up with the world around us through a process of trial and error. In leadership, we can create scenarios where that trial and error is normalized, low-risk, and encouraging. Iterative processes of learning who we are do not need to be utterly painful all the time. Most of us have learned a great deal from our failures, but testing out theories of our traits and the world's factors need not be framed as failure; it is a necessary task for vibrant communities seeking to live out a higher purpose.

The ethics of authenticity. In his book *Forgetting Ourselves on Purpose: Vocation and the Ethics of Ambition*,[60] Brian Mahan provides for us a second form of communal discernment. This book, developed by Mahan out of years of teaching undergraduate

---

[60] Brian J. Mahan, *Forgetting Ourselves on Purpose: Vocation and the Ethics of Ambition* (San Francisco: Jossey-Bass, 2002).

students about the balance they must strike between becoming successful and being fully—authentically—who they are, provides numerous insights regarding discerning our authentic nature. Mahan plays on a common expression in the southern United States, "forgetting ourselves." Where the idiomatic expression refers to a person who has forgotten to use good manners, Mahan uses the expression to describe the sensation we have when we lose track of time and role and live in the moment. Mahan argues that we find our true callings by listening to moments like those and asking ourselves, "What am I doing when I feel entirely myself, unaware of time passing and not desiring to be anyplace else?" He defines authenticity and telling the truth about our desires within an ethical framework, where a trait-factor match is imbued with moral meaning.

If it is true that we should follow our bliss, then we must discern what those activities are, and what they mean. Here *Forgetting Ourselves on Purpose* reminds us that ambition and vocation do not run counter to one another, with ambition being selfish and vocation being worthy. Instead, Mahan points out how ambition and vocation feed into each other and rely on each other. Ambition without vocation sets us up for failure, as it devolves into competitiveness toward no higher purpose; what if someone else succeeds in our area of ambition more impressively than we do? Vocation without ambition leads us to do what we think is noble rather than putting our energies in the places we feel most alive, setting us up to burn out. In other words, there is essential, ethical goodness in discovering what we love to do, and doing it.

The key moment of discovery of vocation, fed by ambition and later energized by it, is what Mahan calls an "epiphany of recruitment."[61] These moments are not always apparent to us, but they clarify who we are and what we are called to do. Yesterday I attended a worship service where one of the students I teach at

---

[61] Mahan, *Forgetting Ourselves on Purpose*, 20.

Yale Divinity School was preaching for the first time in the church that will support him in his ordination process. The pastor and I are both hoping that the church will become an incubator of sorts for aspiring clergy. I was nervous and excited for the student and the church alike; they are in this together. The energy in the service was not just palpable but electrifying. The student preached inspiringly and personally. The faith community rose to the occasion, warmly welcoming the student preacher and all those who came to support him. Did the church discover yesterday that it has a special role to play in the education of clergy? A special bond with the divinity school down the road? Only time will tell, but the emotional dimension of the epiphany of recruitment—the proverbial "a-ha moment"—was certainly present in the sanctuary.

When we are young, we concern ourselves greatly with what others tell us to do and think of us. As we mature, we discover what we love to do and with whom we want to live our lives. This process of maturation involves coming to know ourselves, meeting and learning about other people, and becoming aware of the needs and opportunities in our communities. We can accelerate some of these maturation processes through cultivating habits of discernment. We can also live active, full, and adventuresome lives that speed up the trial and error process through sheer volume of experiences. What we find we love becomes the plumb line that draws us into deeper knowledge of ourselves and the world around us. Acting with integrity means being fully who we are. Analyzing our choices with the question in mind, "Is this *me*? Is this *us*?" is likely to lead us in the right direction.

Theological reflection. A third way in which leaders and their communities make sense of a need for change is by looking through the lens of theology. Faith and reason work together, of course, but overreliance on reason was the sin of the Pharisees. Self-focus and anxiety can distort our perspective. The early Christians were, of course, influenced by the Greek ideal of reason resulting in pure wisdom, but faith is more than reason. It is also more than emotion and power. Faith is not entirely of this earth. Two sets of theological principles can be used to describe faithful discernment toward communal change: Telos versus eschaton, and conversion versus resurrection.

As described in chapter 2, change leadership can begin with a shared process of visioning. Secular resources on change leadership suggest that we use the vision as a plumb line, and although communally derived, the vision belongs to individuals. In such an interpretation, the vision is our telos: the direction toward which we want all work to point us. When we think theologically about visioning, we realize that seeking a vision is not just about knowing our hopes and dreams, but our interpretation of what God wants for creation. The "kingdom," or God's realm, is the world as God envisions it, and our earthly job is to make the world look more like that realm. In this Christian worldview, the achievement of the vision is eschatological—of last things—and represents much more than arrival at a destination. Eschatological change reshapes the world toward God's imagination for it.

Resurrection and conversion are two different ways in which people, and also the institutions people form, are reborn. Jesus died and rose again; Christians believe that Christ died for all of us, and he rose for all of us, ending death itself in doing so. In our lives, we experience resurrections in ways that help us to know of the new life we can find in our faith. We experience heartbreak from which we do not think we can recover, and then we do. We make terrible mistakes that we think will destroy our whole lives, and they do not. Conversion is similar, in that it involves turning away from that which deals death and toward that which gives life. All of these different frameworks help us to look at what might seem a murky situation through the eyes of faith and make better sense of it, and what it is calling on us to do.

Choosing Leadership Approaches

Change leadership is like parenting: parents must multitask as they meet their family's needs. Children need their parents to be authoritative and affectionate, consistent and yet flexible, meeting kids' needs in real-time while also preparing them to be happy and independent adults. Parents who only employ one strategy in raising their children quickly find themselves ineffective and locked in constant conflict. Similarly, leaders who wish to bring about change must be ready to use different strategies as circumstances require. Changing strategies does not make leaders inconsistent or inauthentic; it means they read situations and choose approaches that make sense under the circumstances.

I propose three different directions in which leaders must be ready to turn their attention as they lead change (Figure 5.1). The good news is that they need not face those different directions alone. They not only have colleagues and mentors who can help them, but they also have their physical health, mental sanity, and faith in God that helps them attend to all three directions.

Direction 1: negotiations. Change leaders must pay attention to negotiating the change itself with stakeholders. Many a good opportunity has been lost because of errors in the negotiating process. One bad meeting, a simple misunderstanding, or an unfortunate surprise can be enough to kill even the best idea. Change negotiations bring up identity issues for those we lead, which means that some conflict is inevitable. The negotiations front—which change is best for the organization?—is one that leaders cannot ignore without risking sending the institution on a wild goose chase.

Direction 2: ending well. Change always means bringing old ways to a close, and endings cause grief. As negotiations play out, we must think about how to ensure that those who care about that which is ending are tended to with care and concern. Despite the fact that something is ending so that something else can begin, and the new

FIGURE 5.1

thing might be both exciting and necessary, we must pay attention to grief, or it will go underground and cause pain to individuals and harm to the organization. Those whose churches are merging, for example, must get excited about the new relationships possible but also grieve the loss of individual identities that come with merging. Those whose favorite program is being discontinued in favor of a new direction deserve for that program to be celebrated and honored.

Direction 3: living into the new reality. From the minute an organization makes a decision to move into a new direction, the leaders must look alive. I mean that expression both literally and figuratively: they must get busy in making the change a reality, and they must demonstrate life in the new reality. Those who lose that which is familiar are quick to say that the organization they loved has died. Trying to persuade them otherwise is not likely through words and reason, but acting not-dead just might work.

It is possible, and in fact necessary, to grieve the old *and* start the new *while* negotiating the change. Change means death. It also means life. Holding these two truths at one time, without losing track of the change project, requires multitasking. Living into the new requires planning and teaching, so reason must be engaged. Ending well is rife with emotion; therefore, emotional systems must be taken seriously on that front. Power dynamics shape negotiations more than that which is right, or that which feels emotionally satisfying. And yet in every direction of Figure 5.1, we can see all three dynamics coming into play, not just one. Like the three persons of the Trinity, the three are One, interplaying with each other in ways that cannot be cleanly divided between the functions of a parent, a sibling, and a spirit.

An Illustration of Three Dynamics and Three Leadership Strategies

Again, I consider the professional project in which I have been involved over the past two years: Andover Newton Theological School has become Andover Newton Seminary at Yale Divinity School. I have been part of a group of leaders that has gradually closed our Newton, Massachusetts, campus and gradually opened a new one that is embedded in Yale Divinity School at Yale University. The transition has taken place on all three fronts just described, and each of those fronts involved all three leadership responses, with one at the forefront and the others playing supporting roles.

The negotiations front certainly involved power dynamics. Yale is a big and strong university, and Andover Newton is a small and fragile free-standing seminary. The negotiations involved a fair amount of emotion, too, in that Yale did not want the Andover Newton community at-large to feel negatively about Yale out of grief turned to bitterness, and Yale's leaders realized that a heavy-handed approach would do just that. Similarly, reason was involved every step of the way. Yale wanted to partner with the strongest possible version of Andover Newton, which meant careful planning and educating numerous audiences about the virtues of Andover Newton becoming an embedded institution.

As for ending well, emotional systems would be the obvious perspective to bring to bear in analyzing what is happening and building a leadership strategy. Ending well involved a lot of grieving, and grief is a complex emotion that hits different people in different ways, depending on who they are and what their experiences have been. Those who knew and loved Andover Newton on its Newton campus had a hard time imagining the school being both alive and not there. Much was to be lost. At the same time, that which seemed to alleviate their grief more than any ritual of mourning was seeing that good things were happening in our new location. Emotion was not the only force at work in ending well; reason was important too, and we had to communicate the change. Power dynamics were critical in the process of ending well, as subtle liberationist practices were effective in bringing peace to those involved in the ending: dialogue in the form of support for students and listening to their ideas, humility on the part of trustees (those ultimately responsible for carrying out Andover Newton's mission) for that which they did and did not know, and forums for sharing in grief as well as exchanging ideas for the future.

Starting strong in a new place involved planning and educating, first and foremost. It also, of course, involved emotional self-management—not everything was going to be easy, and we could not give up—and dialogue. Of the three fronts, beginning in the new way well seemed easy in comparison with negotiating and ending that which was historic and ending. I believe this to be true because the main beginning activities related to reason, which I have already argued is closer to the leadership terrain and thus easier to access. The emotions were less complicated, the power dynamics relatively straightforward in our new setting. I came away from the leadership experience more energized as compared with the emotional drain of managing emotions—mine and others'—and the always elusive power dynamics.

Side-Effects Are Manageable When We Are Well

One side-effect of change can be so painful as to cause us to abdicate our responsibility to lead it: conflict. Managing the pain of conflict requires spiritual self-care. This effect/side-effect analysis is particularly timely in this era of new tribalism, where subcultures are digging into bunkers, and conflict is becoming particularly intense. If we avoid change lest we create conflict, we will never lead effectively. Keeping ourselves well in the midst of conflict helps us to teach and plan, to remain separate-yet-together, and to foster dialogue that exposes possibilities.

Conflict Is Something, Not Everything

In the nebulous realm of the leadership terrain, we tend to be hyperaware of the presence of conflict. Some are so averse to it they stay off the leadership terrain altogether. We fear and avoid conflict for good reason: it feels bad. Having skills for facing and working within conflict can help to reduce our anxiety and get us onto the terrain where our leadership is needed. As Peter Block writes in *Community: The Structure of Belonging,* the leader's job is to move a community away from focusing on problems and toward focusing on possibilities.[62] We must meet people where they are and guide them somewhere new. Avoidance of conflict in such cases is tantamount to shirking leadership responsibility.

In the classic romantic comedy "Jerry Maguire,"[63] a sports agent, Jerry, finds himself in conflict with his client, Rod. They discover that Rod comes from a background where conflict among those who care about each other is comfortable and typical. "That's the difference between you and me, Jerry," says Rod. "You think we're fighting, and I think we're finally talking." Rod has a great deal to

---

[62] Block, *Community.*

[63] Cameron Crowe, dir., *Jerry Maguire* (Gracie Films, 1996).

teach Jerry about effective leadership, because fear of conflict paralyzes communication. Each of the leadership practices described in this book relies on communication as a core and key to effectiveness.

A particularly helpful resource for the practice of improving communication comes in the book *Crucial Conversations*,[64] in which Patterson et al. describe a crucial conversation as one where (1) stakes are high, (2) emotions are strong, and (3) reasonable people disagree with one another. When those three dimensions are present, the authors recommend a variety of practices for keeping conversation moving in such a way that it maximizes valid data for decision-making. Note that the goal is not that everyone feel good, but rather that the pool of shared knowledge become enriched.

The practices recommended in *Crucial Conversations* enhance communication rather than setting up a win/lose; conversation is not a sport where one must be victorious over the other. In fact, if increasing shared knowledge is indeed the goal of conversation— why even talk if it is not?—then those who win are those who know more afterward. The book provides a useful set of practices amidst reason, emotion, or power with equal effectiveness. They make room for explaining, making sense, educating, and planning, in that they keep people who are different from one another talking when communication might otherwise break down. They provide the "connected" portion of separate-yet-connected. They make it possible for those with top-down power and grassroots power to find pockets of possibility, as they make space for dialogue when tensions might otherwise suffocate it.

A second resource for keeping conversation flowing came to me from my pastoral care professor at Weston Jesuit School of Theology, Katherine Clark. She advocated what she called the "Sandwich Method," which included "standing for" and

---

64 Kerry Patterson et al., *Crucial Conversations: Tools for Talking When Stakes Are High* (New York: McGraw-Hill, 2012).

"understanding" as the peanut butter and the bread. Sometimes, the leader must approach a tense situation with understanding. Then she must advocate for a position, but in the end she needs to cultivate and demonstrate understanding. Sometimes, understanding and standing-for are inverted: we begin by standing for, then we demonstrate understanding, and we end with reminding the community that for which it stands (Figure 5.2).

Were I to apply this method to a conversation with an Andover Newton alumnus who was unhappy about the closure of our Newton

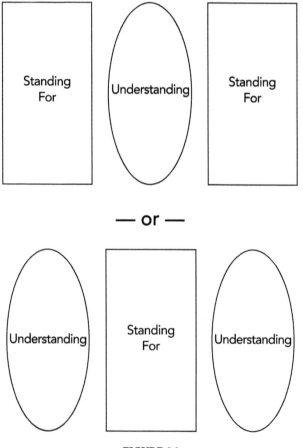

FIGURE 5.2

campus, I might begin with understanding: there is much to grieve, as much had been lost. But I would be remiss not to point out that the change we are making protects and furthers our core mission, and that mission was under serious threat before undertaking a change. I would end the conversation with an understanding word: just because we had to do this and just because closing the campus and opening a new program was our best option, does not make the grief go away. We had something and we lost it. We got something new, to be sure, but the grief is real.

The Sandwich Method employs reason, takes emotion seriously, and uses power to reframe a narrative, taking the interaction out of a competitive mode and into a connective one. So often, leaders try to confront emotion using reason, and they cannot understand why the conversation gets nowhere. The Sandwich Method is a multidisciplinary approach appropriate for a multilayered leadership terrain.

Spiritual Self-Care

So much of leadership has nothing to do with the way we engage others, but the way we manage ourselves: our own emotions and health. We have power shoring us up on all sides, if only we lean into it rather than seeking to go it alone. That power includes an all-powerful God, a support network of colleagues and loved ones, and our physical and mental well-being. When battling on three fronts, the only leader who will last is one who relies on those supports, not just sometimes but all the time.

God is God; whether we worship and adore her or totally ignore her has no impact on her love for us. Yet we know that our adoration and attention to God realigns that which is out of joint in our lives and our leadership. As for me, I go to church. Being part of a congregation and worshiping God is essential to my sense of groundedness. Others have written with far more expertise than I on the connection between leadership effectiveness and spiritual practice, but as for me, regular worship is less about effectiveness and more about not losing track of who and whose I am.

Collegial bonds have become increasingly important in my life, probably because I now have more colleagues than I once did, spread out among other theological schools. I keep a folder in my email box labeled "colleagues," and if I go more than a day without putting something in it, I reach out to colleagues myself. In addition to peers with roles similar to my own, I make a point of keeping in close touch with my five closest women friends. Three from college, one from graduate school, and one from ministry: we all have spouses, kids, careers, and a sense of humor. I rarely let a week go by without touching base with each of them about something going on in their lives or mine.

Embodiment is utterly essential to effective leadership. Our bodies are not just where our souls live; they are part of our souls. Strong bodies, frail bodies, young bodies, old bodies: a key to grounded leadership is that we have bodies. By taking care of our bodies and our minds, we are constantly reminding ourselves that we are whole. We are not fused, like one would see in a sick system, with our workplaces or communities. We are separate-yet-together with them. When we are able to think clearly, we see clearly, making reasoned decisions and communicating them well. Each of the three dimensions of change leadership relies on our physical, mental, and spiritual health. Reason requires our sanity, emotion requires us to be well enough to maintain boundaries, power dynamics require us to manage stress. We are learning along with science that there is little difference between the physical and mental when it comes to what hurts and what heals, so we must care of our brains as part of our bodies in order to lead.

We find evidence of adequate self-care in the form of healthy boundaries. Role confusion is a nearly inevitable side effect of poor self-care. Remembering who we are to others and whose responsibility it is to meet our needs is almost impossible when we have lost track of what makes us whole. In addition to worshiping God, leaning on friends, and caring for our minds and bodies, practices of emotional self-management help us to remain attuned to the leadership needs of the situations in which we find ourselves. The noise of our own needs can otherwise drown out the sounds of a leadership situation asking for our attention. Healthy boundaries and prayerful body awareness in real time are two ways in which we can wade into the fast-moving waters of stress and conflict without being swept away.

Boundaries are the rules we set about how we will conduct ourselves and how we will allow ourselves to be treated. We use them in part to take care of ourselves, but even more importantly, boundaries correct the power differentials between ourselves and those whom we serve, protecting them from us.[65] We set boundaries by creating simple policies for ourselves that guide our behavior. A good set of boundaries make us mindful of who is our "client"— those whom it is our role to serve—and whose are meant to be serving us.[66] We are allowed to take satisfaction from our clients' flourishing, but we do not use them for our own pleasure. We are permitted to receive remuneration in the form of compensation for work done well, but we are not to be remunerated in the form of the titillating gossip that results from breached confidentiality.

Boundaries get muddiest when we are burned out. Conversely, poor boundaries are a recipe for burnout (see chapter 3). Those who suffer from work-related depression, or burnout, have labored under unrealistic expectations and do not enjoy a connection between hard work and success. Think of a time in your life when you have cared deeply about the results of a decision over which you had no power, and you can hearken up feelings of both helplessness and

---

[65] I learned this definition of boundaries—the rules we set to ensure justice amidst power differentials—over ten years of ongoing learning with Marie Fortune of the Faith-Trust Institute.

[66] Elaine Peterson, *At Personal Risk: Boundary Violations in Professional-Client Relationships* (New York: Norton, 1992).

frustration, two emotions that do not support your best separate-yet-togetherness. Frustration that a challenge requires our maximal effort? A break or a good night's sleep will usually do the trick. Frustration that our challenge is to watch and wait, helplessly and indefinitely? Burnout is likely to ensue. We can prevent or fight burnout by placing realistic expectations on ourselves, even if our workplace is not going to do that for us. We can maintain perspective best when we have a strong sense of identity beyond our work.

Early in my career, I met two different men who had been pushed out of jobs in educational institutions. Each man carried wounds that seemed like they were just beginning to heal, so when I learned they had lost those previous jobs decades earlier, these revelations got my attention. Everyone processes grief differently and at different paces, of course, but these men's protracted sense of anger, bitterness, and having been done wrong served for me as a cautionary tale. How might I—how might we—cultivate a working life where we expect less of institutions and expect more by way of happiness from that which lies within us? How can I develop the ego strength whereby bad endings to professional roles cannot shake me to the deepest foundation, disappointing and upsetting as such experiences can be?

In all these experiences, from boundaries to burnout, we are mindful that God, our support network, and our health are all essential to our integrity—our wholeness. Change leadership cannot be done from a shaky scaffold. When we are seeking to lead change, we have to be ready to destabilize the institution we serve while making the moves that ensure a more satisfactory stability. If the entirety of our identity rests on the institution as it is, we will not have the ego fortitude to make the changes that need to happen.

I recently attended a talk by David Swenson, who leads the team that invests Yale University's endowment. The talk was during reunion weekend, and Swenson arrived with an over-the-top school spirit blazer that had been given to him as a gift; he looked like he could have been on the cheerleading squad at the Yale-Harvard football game. He spoke about how he entered his work at Yale seeking a return to first principles: what is an endowment, and what is it supposed to do for the institution it supports? He embodied a separate-yet-togetherness. He was able to get perspective on the purpose of his team without getting sucked into "how we have always done things." Simultaneously, he demonstrated school spirit and boosterism, clearly motivated by love. He made a joke during his talk about how when the endowment growth was strong, his strategy was called "The Yale Plan," and when it was imperiled such as during the market crisis of 2008, it was called "The Swenson Plan." He got a good laugh for that joke. That his ego and identity could survive these fluctuations in reputation, making them seem ordinary rather than tragic, signaled healthy mental state.

Spiritual Practices for Integration

Here is the good news: none of us is born fully integrated in our faith, relationships, and health. We have the capacity to grow and improve and mature in this integration, learning from experience and cultivating spiritual practices that promote such integration. Two examples of spiritual practices that help us to stay on solid ground while facing change leadership are sacred mantras and welcoming prayer.

Mantras are short phrases associated with meditative practices. The repetition of sacred words brings us back to ourselves when we might otherwise become consumed by the stress around us amidst change. One mantra that has been particularly helpful to me over the years, shared with me by a friend quoting her spiritual director, is "breathe in with the word 'proportion'; breathe out with the word 'perspective.'" Three rounds of this mantra when I am surrounded by those who are losing their heads is usually enough to keep mine attached. Outside of the leadership context, such practices are important for staying grounded and separate-yet-together with our communities.

I have deep respect for those who practice meditation and centering prayer, which is meditation using a sacred word to hold our attention. In the midst of leadership, I have found more help in the practice of welcoming prayer, centering prayer's action-oriented corollary.[67] If we believe that God's will is made known to us through our emotions, as the Jesuits do; and if we believe that our emotions are located only partly in our brain but also partly in our bodies, which scientists are starting to understand; then listening to our bodies in the midst of tension is important, for our bodies are telling us what God would have us do.

Welcoming prayer takes bodily location of emotions seriously. It also takes seriously that we carry anxieties from our childhood that no longer serve us as adults but that, even in their vestigial nature, can disrupt our peace of mind. The practice works like this: when we experience a wave of anxiety, we seek to locate it in our body. Do I feel tightness in my chest, or has a pit appeared in my stomach? We find the feeling and say to it, "Welcome," for we know that the sensation is trying to tell us something we need to know. We sink into the feeling rather than trying to push it away.

After sinking in, even if just for a moment, we let the feeling dissipate, sending it off with four releases, each related to a childhood anxiety no longer serving us well, saying,

1. "I release my need for power and control."
2. "I release my need for safety and security."
3. "I release my need for love and esteem."
4. "I release my need to change any of this."

---

[67] I learned the practice of centering prayer from my spiritual director, Barbara Prendergast, when I lived in Milwaukee. She encouraged me to attend a workshop on welcoming prayer with Mary Dwyer, whose teachings are reflected in my description here.

Sometimes we go through this entire process while still participating in the meeting that is causing us stress. Over time, I have found that different parts of my body are associated with different vestigial needs, and, therefore, I have been able to work on those anxieties when I am away from the leadership terrain.

Closing Thoughts

Over the past year, I have discovered many ways in which a multidisciplinary approach to change leadership is useful. I have become increasingly annoyed at the same time with those who seek to oversimplify change leadership, making it sound easy in an effort to shame leaders who have trouble carrying it off. I have also discovered limitations of a multidisciplinary approach. The leadership terrain is not a golf course, where we can choose our club based on the lie of the ball. We sometimes have to golf blind, on unfamiliar grass, with an obstructed view of the hole.

If at any point this book seemed to make change seem simple, I either worded something wrong, or you read something wrong. It is not. If at any point change sounded just too hard, that is probably closer to the truth, but not right either. If you are finishing this book thinking that change is complicated, but altogether possible to lead well, then my work here is done, and yours is about to begin.

Acknowledgements

As this book comes to a close, I would like to extend my thanks to Martin Copenhaver, my colleague and friend. Were it not for Martin, this book simply would not have been possible. The ideas would not have had the chance to come to maturity were we not working together. The time, space, and encouragement he offered over our years of colleagueship left me with no excuses: I had to take on this project. I am most grateful for the many times Martin and I have agreed that everyone was crazy, "but for me and thee." I also wish to thank Dean Gregory S. Sterling and the Andover Newton Trustees for supporting a sabbatical that made the writing of this book possible.

Finally, and always, I extend my thanksgiving to my spouse, Daniel Birmingham Drummond, and our daughter, J.J., who have made changes in their own lives to make possible the moves about which I write in this book. They fill my life with love and laughter.

Bibliography

Bass, Dorothy, and Miroslav Volf. "A Theological Understanding of Christian Practices." In *Practicing Theology: Beliefs and Practices in Christian Life*, 13–32. Grand Rapids, MI: Eerdmans, 2002.

Bendroth, Margaret. *The Last Puritans: Mainline Protestants and the Power of the Past*. Chapel Hill: University of North Carolina Press, 2015.

Block, Peter. *Community: The Structure of Belonging*. San Francisco: Berrett-Koehler , 2008.

Boal, Agusto. *The Rainbow of Desire: The Boal Method of Theatre and Therapy*. Translated by Adrian Jackson. London and New York: Routledge, 1995.

Boers, Arthur. *Never Call Them Jerks*. Bethesda, MD: Alban Institute, 1999.

Brest, Paul. "The Power of Theories of Change." *Stanford Social Innovation Review*, Spring 2010, 47–51.

Carroll, Jackson W. *God's Potters: Pastoral Leadership and the Shaping of Congregations*. Grand Rapids, MI: Eerdmans, 2006.

Cormode, Scott. *Making Spiritual Sense: Christian Leaders as Spiritual Interpreters*. Nashville: Abingdon Press, 2006.

Crowe, Cameron, dir. "Jerry Maguire." Gracie Films, 1996.

Daloz Parks, Sharon. *Leadership Can Be Taught: A Bold Approach for a Complex World*. Boston: Harvard Business School Press, 2005.

Desmond, Matthew. *Evicted: Poverty and Profit in the American City*. Milan: Daily Books, 2017.

Drummond, Sarah. *Holy Clarity: The Practice of Planning and Evaluation*. Herndon, VA: Alban Institute, 2009.

Eisenstat, Russel, Bert Spector, and Michael Beer. "Why Change Programs Don't Produce Change." *Harvard Business Review*, no. 11 (November–December, 1990).

Fackre, Gabriel. *Believing, Caring, and Doing in the United Church of Christ.* Cleveland: United Church Press, 2005.

Forti, Matthew. "Six Theory of Change Pitfalls to Avoid." *Stanford Social Innovation Review,* May 23, 2012.

Freire, Paolo. *Pedagogy of the Oppressed.* New York: Continuum, 1997. 1970.

Friedman, Edwin. *A Failure of Nerve: Leadership in the Age of the Quick Fix.* New York: Church Publishing, 1999, 2007.

————. *Generation to Generation: Family Process in Church and Synagogue.* New York: Guilford Press, 1985.

Galluzzo, Gregory. "Faith-Based Organizing—a Justice Ministry: A Strategy for Ministry." *International Journal of Public Theology* 3 (2009): 108–14.

Gardner, Lee. "Faculty on Board: The Subtle Art of Gaining Faculty Buy-In." *The Chronicle of Higher Education,* June 23, 2017.

Heifetz, Ronald A. *Leadership without Easy Answers.* Cambridge, MA: Harvard University Press, 1994.

Hirschman, Albert O. *Exit, Voice, and Loyalty: Responses to Decline in Firms, Organizations, and States.* Cambridge, MA: Harvard University Press, 1970.

Jones, L. Gregory, and Kevin R. Armstrong. *Resurrecting Excellence: Shaping Faithful Christian Ministry.* Grand Rapids, MI: Eerdmans, 2006.

Kegan, Robert. *The Evolving Self: Problem and Process in Human Development.* Cambridge, MA: Harvard University Press, 1982.

Kegan, Robert, and Lisa Laskow Lahey. *Immunity to Change: How to Overcome It and Unlock the Potential in Yourself and Your Organization.* Boston: Harvard University Press, 2009.

Kotter, John P. *Leading Change.* Boston: Harvard Business School Press, 1996.

Mahan, Brian J. *Forgetting Ourselves on Purpose: Vocation and the Ethics of Ambition.* San Francisco: Jossey-Bass, 2002.

Marsden, George M. *A Short Life of Jonathan Edwards.* Grand Rapids, MI: Eerdmans, 2008.

Norheim, Bård Eirik Hallesby. "A Grain of Wheat: Toward a Theological Anthropology for Leading Change in Ministry." *Journal of Religious Leadership.* Vol. 13, No. 1 (Spring 2014): 68–77.

Outka, Gene. *Agape: An Ethical Analysis*. New Haven, CT: Yale University Press, 1972.

Palmer, Parker J. *The Active Life: A Spirituality of Work, Creativity, and Caring*. San Francisco: Jossey-Bass, 1999.

Palmer, Parker J. *The Courage to Teach*. San Francisco: Jossey-Bass, 1998.

Patterson, Kerry, et al. *Crucial Conversations: Tools for Talking When Stakes Are High*. New York: McGraw-Hill, 2012.

Peterson, Elaine. *At Personal Risk: Boundary Violations in Professional-Client Relationships*. New York: Norton, 1992.

Ste-Marie, Lorraine. ""Immunity-to-Change Language Technology": An Educational Tool for Pastoral Leadership Education." *Teaching Theology and Religion* 11, no. 2 (2008): 92–102.

Thornton, Sharon Garred. *Broken yet Beloved*. St. Louis, MO: Chalice Press, 2002.

"Undercover Boss." CBS, television series, 2010.